THE MEANING OF JACKSONIAN DEMOCRACY

Problems in American Civilization

UNDER THE EDITORIAL DIRECTION OF *George Rogers Taylor*

THE MEANING OF
JACKSONIAN DEMOCRACY

EDITED WITH AN INTRODUCTION BY
Edwin C. Rozwenc

AMHERST COLLEGE

Problems in American Civilization

D. C. HEATH AND COMPANY: Boston

INTRODUCTION

"JACKSONIAN democracy" is a conventional term that most historians use without much thought about its validity as a historical concept. No student of American historiography has been able to establish with any degree of certainty who invented this generalizing term, but a perusal of some of the standard historical writings indicates that the concept became an accepted part of the historian's vocabulary in the twentieth century. Such leading historians of the late nineteenth century, as Von Holst, Schouler, and McMaster, for example, had not used the concept. All three in varying ways betrayed their allegiance to the Whiggish conception of "the reign of King Andrew" in their interpretations of the 1830's.

In the decade before World War I, when American historians and social scientists were contributing to the criticism and reform of social ills in American life, the American past was re-examined and rewritten in order to give the progressive ideology some grounding in historical truth. The Jacksonian period began to take on a new significance as a time of social conflict and of a striving toward democratic reforms. Thus, Woodrow Wilson, in his *History of the American People* (1901), entitled his opening chapter on the Jacksonian administrations "The Democratic Revolution." When the *American Nation* series was launched in 1906, the volume on the Jacksonian period written by William MacDonald was boldly entitled "Jacksonian Democ-

racy." Frederick Jackson Turner gave added significance to the concept in one of his essays written for the *Mississippi Valley Historical Review* in 1909.

Herbert Croly wove the new historical conception into the fabric of progressive thought when he made it a matter of serious inquiry in *The Promise of American Life* (1910). Indeed, Croly asserted that, despite their narrowness and negativism in the use of national power, the Jacksonian democrats had been the first large body of Americans to be genuinely democratic in feeling and the first to give genuine social vitality to the democratic ideal in American life.

Inasmuch as the idea of democracy has developed an even stronger value for Americans in the succeeding decades of the twentieth century, it should not surprise us that a considerable amount of historical scholarship has continued to be directed toward attempts to identify the social groups that supported the Jacksonian movement and to explain the forces that shaped it. Thus, some historians have emphasized that Jacksonian democracy was primarily an outgrowth of the pioneer democracy of the newer states of the West and Southwest. Others have maintained that the social goals of Jacksonian democracy were shaped by the social pressures of the rapidly changing economic order in the older states of the East. All in all, a great many words have been written to demonstrate that the essential core of Jacksonianism is to be found either among urban workingmen or among backwoods farmers or among eager entrepreneurs.

There were some twentieth-century writers, however, who were disinclined to accept the concept of Jacksonian democracy as central to a synthesis of the period. In his volume for the *History of American Life* series, Carl Russell Fish preferred "the age of the common man" as a more inclusive generalizing term for the great variety of forms in which the egalitarian urges of America in the period from 1830 to 1850 expressed themselves when he wrote his volume for the *History of American Life* series. Louis Hartz saw the Jacksonian era as part of the continuing philosophic confusion in the liberal tradition of American thought between the Revolution and the Civil War. More recently, Lee Benson has proclaimed the necessity for discarding the concept of Jacksonian democracy and has proposed "the age of egalitarianism" as a synthesizing term that would be less likely to lead the historian to distort reality.[1]

We must certainly acknowledge that most of the changes in suffrage and office-holding qualifications which established more democratic electoral procedures for adult white males in the United States were introduced before the Jacksonian democrats controlled the centers of decision-making power. Other political groups were as active as Jacksonian democrats, and sometimes more so, in introducing some of the new popular devices of nomination and election. Moreover, George Rogers Taylor has demonstrated very effectively that "the transportation revolution" stimulated and accelerated social and economic changes

between 1815 and 1860 and that these changes took place no matter who was in the White House or which party controlled Congress.[2] Hence there may be considerable justification for rejecting the concept of Jacksonian democracy as useful for the purposes of historical synthesis.

On the other hand, we must recognize that the economic and social changes which accompanied "the transportation revolution" did not necessarily guarantee a transformation in America from the liberal, aristocratic republic of the early nineteenth century to an egalitarian democracy by the mid-nineteenth century. In the experience of other nations, the take-off phase of industrial development has often been accompanied by an intensification of the disparities of wealth and the inequalities of status. Therefore, we need to ask ourselves what there was in the American social situation that made the rapid economic growth of the first stage of our industrial revolution go hand in hand with egalitarian social conditions. And it is when we raise this question that we find ourselves confronting the concept of Jacksonian democracy in a more necessitous way.

Certainly we cannot fall back on the comfortable assumption that the changes in voting and officeholding qualifications were of themselves creating an egalitarian democracy. Voter participation did not rise automatically with the changes in the electoral laws. Yet, with the help of Richard McCormick's analysis, we do know that, between 1828 and 1840, the national average of voter participation in presidential elections always stayed close to the highest levels of voter turnout that had ever been attained in the

[1] See Lee Benson, *The Concept of Jacksonian Democracy, New York as a Test Case* (Princeton, 1961). Especially Ch. XV.

[2] See George Rogers Taylor, *The Transportation Revolution* (New York, 1951).

first quarter of the nineteenth century. And, in 1840, the surge to the polls exceeded previous peaks of voter participation in the majority of the states.[3] A mighty democratic uprising had certainly taken place in national politics in the Jacksonian decade and continued apace in the 1840's.

It would be difficult to explain such changes in American political behavior without taking into account the new intensity of party conflict created by the Jacksonian democrats. Part of this increase in voter interest undoubtedly was a response to Andrew Jackson himself; "Old Hero" certainly was a symbol for the age. But we must also assume that the actions of the Jacksonians made the party battles of the 1830's and 1840's a consuming passion. By word and by deed, Jackson transformed the Presidency and laid the foundation for the future expansion of executive power. Moreover, Andrew Jackson created a commanding presidential voice which dramatized important social goals and defined the terms of the basic political dialogue for his generation. In addition, the Jacksonians organized on a national scale the techniques of mass politics already developed in the states, and forced the Whigs to adopt the same techniques in order to be politically successful.

The readings in this volume have been chosen to help us re-examine the concept of Jacksonian democracy. Since the historical interpretation of the more remote past comes out of a peculiar dialogue between the living and the dead, the readings in this volume are arranged in two chronological groups. The first group of selections represents the articu-

lations of men and women of the Jacksonian generation as they attempted to give a meaning to their own social experience. The second group is made up of selections from the writings of twentieth-century historians who are using the historical perspectives of our century to explain the significance of the changes in the second quarter of the nineteenth century.

The first selection, appropriately, is a statement of political principles by Andrew Jackson given to the American people in his Farewell Address in 1837. This is followed by a more philosophic essay on the natural wisdom of the common man, written by George Bancroft, a leading Jacksonian intellectual. Then, the opening editorial in the *Democratic Review* gives us something like a codification of democratic principles by a leading journal of Democratic opinion. The subsequent editorial by Orestes Brownson provides us with some understanding of the thinking of the radical, Loco-Foco, wing of the Democratic party.

Then follow two statements by Whig leaders. One is a summation of Whig principles made by Henry Clay in 1840. The other is a tract on capital and labor written in 1844 by Calvin Colton, a leading Whig editor. These two selections can give us some idea of the perspective of the Whigs as they tried to give meaning to their social experience during the Jacksonian generation.

Finally, the first group of selections includes some comments about American politics and society by three Europeans —Alexis de Tocqueville, Harriet Martineau, and Francis Grund. These selections offer us an interpretation of American attitudes and behavior in the Jacksonian era by contemporary observers whose European backgrounds gave them

[3] See Richard P. McCormick, "New Perspectives on Jacksonian Politics," *American Historical Review* (January 1960), LXV, 288–301.

a more detached perspective.

In the second group of selections, we begin with Frederick Jackson Turner's interpretation of Jacksonian democracy. As we might expect, he emphasizes the influence of frontier democracy in the development of Jacksonian democracy. The selection from Arthur Meier Schlesinger, Jr., *The Age of Jackson,* develops his thesis that eastern workingmen and eastern intellectuals shaped the goals of Jacksonian democracy. In the next selection, Richard Hofstadter seeks to establish a link between Andrew Jackson and the forces of liberal capitalism. Bray Hammond develops this thesis further by demonstrating the connections between leading Jacksonians and state bankers and other businessmen.

In the final selections, our attention is focused much more on the qualities of mind and on some of the inner psychic conflicts of the Jacksonian generation. Louis Hartz examines the inner tensions and the philosophic confusion of "the American Democrat." The selection by Marvin Meyers summarizes many of the essential points of his careful analysis of "the Jacksonian persuasion."

When we have read all of these selections we are in a better position to raise further questions about the meaning of Jacksonian democracy. How did the Jacksonians themselves conceive of the democratic character of their social experience? In what ways did they attempt to shape the social goals of a democratic America? How does the Whig view of the Jacksonian decade differ from that of the Jacksonian Democrats? Do the Whigs and Democrats share any basic assumptions and values? What do the detached perspectives of the European observers enable us to see more clearly about Jack-

sonian America than we can with the statements of either the Jacksonians or the Whigs?

As we reflect about the various interpretations by twentieth-century historians, we need to ask ourselves whether we can identify with any clarity the social groups that supported the Jacksonian movement. Does it really make any difference to say that the support of the Jacksonians came primarily from urban workingmen, backwoods farmers, or eager entrepreneurs, or is there some way in which all three groups function with similar patterns of behavior and similar social goals? What do twentieth-century historians add to an understanding of the Jacksonian generation that we cannot get from the statements made by the various representatives of the Jacksonian generation? Is Jacksonian democracy to be considered mainly as an affair of party politics or as a broad political, social, and intellectual movement? If we think of it in the latter sense, is "Jacksonian Democracy" a useful concept for explaining these broader social and intellectual movements?

To probe the meaning of Jacksonian democracy in this way is to discover more about ourselves. No people can live without a sense of history, without a tradition which gives some direction and meaning to cultural experience. Sophisticated Americans in the second half of the twentieth century can continue to assess the weakness and strength of our democratic national character only by understanding its historical groundwork. We, too, may reshape our conception of proper democratic goals, as Herbert Croly and the progressive generation did when they reexamined the Jacksonian period of American history.

CONTENTS

THE CLASH OF ISSUES

Andrew Jackson described his own era in the following terms:

> . . . from the earliest ages of history to the present day there never have been thirteen millions of people associated in one political body who enjoyed so much freedom and happiness as the people of these United States. You have no longer any cause to fear danger from abroad . . . It is from within, among yourselves—from cupidity, from corruption, from disappointed ambition and inordinate thirst for power—that factions will be formed and liberty endangered. . . .

The Whig editor and political economist, Calvin Colton, chose to emphasize these characteristics of the Jacksonian generation:

> Ours is a country, where men start from an humble origin, and from small beginnings rise gradually in the world, as the reward of merit and industry, and where they attain to the most elevated positions, or acquire a large amount of wealth, according to the pursuits they elect for themselves. No exclusive privileges of birth, no entailment of estates, no civil or political disqualifications, stand in their path; but one has as good a chance as another, according to his talents, prudence, and personal exertions. This is a country of *self-made men*, than which nothing better could be said of any state of society.

Writing a century later, Frederick Jackson Turner declared:

> Jacksonian Democracy was based primarily upon the characteristics of the back country. Jackson himself was a product of the frontier West. . . .

But Arthur M. Schlesinger, Jr., described the main orientation of Jacksonian economic policy in the following terms:

> By origin and interest, it was a policy which appealed mainly to the submerged classes of the East and to farmers of the South rather than to the frontier. Historians have too long been misled by the tableau of Jackson, the wild backwoodsman, erupting into the White House. . . .

Bray Hammond, however, sees a different class of interests behind Jacksonian policies:

> Nothwithstanding their language . . . the Jacksonians' destruction of the Bank of the United States was in no sense a blow at capitalism or property or the "money power." It was a blow at an older set of capitalists by a newer, more numerous set. It was . . . the transfer of primacy from an old, conservative merchant class to a newer, more aggressive, and more numerous body of business men and speculators of all sorts.

Marvin Meyers insists that the Jacksonian democracy can best be under-stood as an inner conflict between the desires and the ideals of the Jack-sonian generation:

> In this direction one can begin to meet the Jacksonian paradox: the fact that the movement which helped to clear the path for laissez-faire capitalism and its culture in America, and the public which in its daily life eagerly entered on that path, held nevertheless in their political conscience an ideal of a chaste republican order, resisting the seductions of risk and novelty, greed and extravagance, rapid motion and complex dealings.

I. THE PERSPECTIVES OF THE JACKSONIAN GENERATION

A. THE JACKSONIANS

Andrew Jackson: THE CAUSE OF FREEDOM WILL CONTINUE TO TRIUMPH OVER ALL ITS ENEMIES

Andrew Jackson's Farewell Address (March 4, 1837) constitutes a summing up of his political principles, refined and hardened in the fierce heat of political controversy during his eight years in the Presidency. In this address, we find his conceptions of such key symbols as the Constitution and the Union. In addition, we can discover his ideas about the proper use of governmental power and his warnings about the evils which must be removed in order to maintain the good habits and the proper moral tone of a free society.

FELLOW-CITIZENS: Being about to retire finally from public life, I beg leave to offer you my grateful thanks for the many proofs of kindness and confidence which I have received at your hands. It has been my fortune in the discharge of public duties, civil and military, frequently to have found myself in difficult and trying situations, where prompt decision and energetic action were necessary, and where the interest of the country required that high responsibilities should be fearlessly encountered; and it is with the deepest emotions of gratitude that I acknowledge the continued and unbroken confidence with which you have sustained me in every trial. My public life has been a long one, and I cannot hope that it has at all times been free from errors; but I have the consolation of knowing that if mistakes have been committed, they have not seriously injured the country I

so anxiously endeavored to serve, and at the moment when I surrender my last public trust I leave this great people prosperous and happy, in the full enjoyment of liberty and peace, and honored and respected by every nation of the world.

If my humble efforts have in any degree contributed to preserve to you these blessings, I have been more than rewarded by the honors you have heaped upon me, and, above all, by the generous confidence with which you have supported me in every peril, and with which you have continued to animate and cheer my path to the closing hour of my political life. The time has now come when advanced age and a broken frame warn me to retire from public concerns, but the recollection of the many favors you have bestowed upon me is engraven upon my heart, and I have felt that I could not part from your service without

From Andrew Jackson's Farewell Address, in James D. Richardson's, *A Compilation of the Messages and Papers of the Presidents, 1789–1897,* Washington, D.C., 1896, Vol. III, pp. 292–306.

making this public acknowledgment of the gratitude I owe you. And if I use the occasion to offer to you the counsels of age and experience, you will, I trust, receive them with the same indulgent kindness which you have so often extended to me, and will at least see in them an earnest desire to perpetuate in this favored land the blessings of liberty and equal law.

We have now lived almost fifty years under the Constitution framed by the sages and patriots of the Revolution. The conflicts in which the nations of Europe were engaged during a great part of this period, the spirit in which they waged war against each other, and our intimate commerical connections with every part of the civilized world rendered it a time of much difficulty for the Government of the United States. We have had our seasons of peace and of war, with all the evils which precede or follow a state of hostility with powerful nations. We encountered these trials with our Constitution yet in its infancy, and under the disadvantages which a new and untried government must always feel when it is called upon to put forth its whole strength without the lights of experience to guide it or the weight of precedents to justify its measures. But we have passed triumphantly through all these difficulties. Our Constitution is no longer a doubtful experiment, and at the end of nearly half a century we find that it has preserved unimpaired the liberties of the people, secured the rights of property, and that our country has improved and is flourishing beyond any former example in the history of nations.

In our domestic concerns there is everything to encourage us, and if you are true to yourselves nothing can impede your march to the highest point of national prosperity. The States which had so long been retarded in their improvement by the Indian tribes residing in the midst of them are at length relieved from the evil, and this unhappy race—the original dwellers in our land—are now placed in a situation where we may well hope that they will share in the blessings of civilization and be saved from that degradation and destruction to which they were rapidly hastening while they remained in the States; and while the safety and comfort of our own citizens have been greatly promoted by their removal, the philanthropist will rejoice that the remnant of that ill-fated race has been at length placed beyond the reach of injury or oppression, and that the paternal care of the General Government will hereafter watch over them and protect them.

If we turn to our relations with foreign powers, we find our condition equally gratifying. Actuated by the sincere desire to do justice to every nation and to preserve the blessings of peace, our intercourse with them has been conducted on the part of this Government in the spirit of frankness; and I take pleasure in saying that it has generally been met in a corresponding temper. Difficulties of old standing have been surmounted by friendly discussion and the mutual desire to be just, and the claims of our citizens, which had been long withheld, have at length been acknowledged and adjusted and satisfactory arrangements made for their final payment; and with a limited, and I trust a temporary, exception, our relations with every foreign power are now of the most friendly character, our commerce continually expanding, and our flag respected in every quarter of the world.

These cheering and grateful prospects and these multiplied favors we owe, under Providence, to the adoption of the

Federal Constitution. It is no longer a question whether this great country can remain happily united and flourish under our present form of government. Experience, the unerring test of all human undertakings, has shown the wisdom and foresight of those who formed it, and has proved that in the union of these States there is a sure foundation for the brightest hopes of freedom and for the happiness of the people. At every hazard and by every sacrifice this Union must be preserved.

The necessity of watching with jealous anxiety for the preservation of the Union was earnestly pressed upon his fellow-citizens by the Father of his Country in his Farewell Address. He has there told us that "while experience shall not have demonstrated its impracticability, there will always be reason to distrust the patriotism of those who in any quarter may endeavor to weaken its bands"; and he has cautioned us in the strongest terms against the formation of parties on geographical discriminations, as one of the means which might disturb our Union and to which designing men would be likely to resort.

The lessons contained in this invaluable legacy of Washington to his countrymen should be cherished in the heart of every citizen to the latest generation; and perhaps at no period of time could they be more usefully remembered than at the present moment; for when we look upon the scenes that are passing around us and dwell upon the pages of his parting address, his paternal counsels would seem to be not merely the offspring of wisdom and foresight, but the voice of prophecy, foretelling events and warning us of the evil to come. Forty years have passed since this imperishable document was given to his countrymen. The Federal Constitution was then regarded by

him as an experiment—and he so speaks of it in his Address—but an experiment upon the success of which the best hopes of his country depended; and we all know that he was prepared to lay down his life, if necessary, to secure to it a full and a fair trial. The trial has been made. It has succeeded beyond the proudest hopes of those who framed it. Every quarter of this widely extended nation has felt its blessings and shared in the general prosperity produced by its adoption. But amid this general prosperity and splendid success the dangers of which he warned us are becoming every day more evident, and the signs of evil are sufficiently apparent to awaken the deepest anxiety in the bosom of the patriot. We behold systematic efforts publicly made to sow the seeds of discord between different parts of the United States and to place party divisions directly upon geographical distinctions; to excite the *South* against the *North* and the *North* against the *South,* and to force into the controversy the most delicate and exciting topics—topics upon which it is impossible that a large portion of the Union can ever speak without strong emotion. Appeals, too, are constantly made to sectional interests in order to influence the election of the Chief Magistrate, as if it were desired that he should favor a particular quarter of the country instead of fulfilling the duties of his station with impartial justice to all; and the possible dissolution of the Union has at length become an ordinary and familiar subject of discussion. Has the warning voice of Washington been forgotten, or have designs already been formed to sever the Union? Let it not be supposed that I impute to all of those who have taken an active part in these unwise and unprofitable discussions a want of patriotism or of public virtue. The honorable feeling of State pride and local attachments finds a place in the bosoms of the most enlightened and pure. But while such men are conscious of their own integrity and honesty of purpose, they ought never to forget that the citizens of other States are their political brethren, and that however mistaken they may be in their views, the great body of them are equally honest and upright with themselves. Mutual suspicions and reproaches may in time create mutual hostility, and artful and designing men will always be found who are ready to foment these fatal divisions and to inflame the natural jealousies of different sections of the country. The history of the world is full of such examples, and especially the history of republics.

What have you to gain by division and dissension? Delude not yourselves with the belief that a breach once made may be afterwards repaired. If the Union is once severed, the line of separation will grow wider and wider, and the controversies which are now debated and settled in the halls of legislation will then be tried in fields of battle and determined by the sword. Neither should you deceive yourselves with the hope that the first line of separation would be the permanent one, and that nothing but harmony and concord would be found in the new associations formed upon the dissolution of this Union. Local interests would still be found there, and unchastened ambition. And if the recollection of common dangers, in which the people of these United States stood side by side against the common foe, the memory of victories won by their united valor, the prosperity and happiness they have enjoyed under the present Constitution, the proud name they bear as citizens of this great Republic—if all these recollections and proofs of common interest are

not strong enough to bind us together as one people, what tie will hold united the new divisions of empire when these bonds have been broken and this Union dissevered? The first line of separation would not last for a single generation; new fragments would be torn off, new leaders would spring up, and this great and glorious Republic would soon be broken into a multitude of petty States, without commerce, without credit, jealous of one another, armed for mutual aggression, loaded with taxes to pay armies and leaders, seeking aid against each other from foreign powers, insulted and trampled upon by the nations of Europe, until, harassed with conflicts and humbled and debased in spirit, they would be ready to submit to the absolute dominion of any military adventurer and to surrender their liberty for the sake of repose. It is impossible to look on the consequences that would inevitably follow the destruction of this Government and not feel indignant when we hear cold calculations about the value of the Union and have so constantly before us a line of conduct so well calculated to weaken its ties.

There is too much at stake to allow pride or passion to influence your decision. Never for a moment believe that the great body of the citizens of any State or States can deliberately intend to do wrong. They may, under the influence of temporary excitement or misguided opinions, commit mistakes; they may be misled for a time by the suggestions of self-interest; but in a community so enlightened and patriotic as the people of the United States argument will soon make them sensible of their errors, and when convinced they will be ready to repair them. If they have no higher or better motives to govern them, they will at least perceive that their own interest requires them to be just to others, as they hope to receive justice at their hands.

But in order to maintain the Union unimpaired it is absolutely necessary that the laws passed by the constituted authorities should be faithfully executed in every part of the country, and that every good citizen should at all times stand ready to put down, with the combined force of the nation, every attempt at unlawful resistance, under whatever pretext it may be made or whatever shape it may assume. Unconstitutional or oppressive laws may no doubt be passed by Congress, either from erroneous views or the want of due consideration; if they are within the reach of judicial authority, the remedy is easy and peaceful; and if, from the character of the law, it is an abuse of power not within the control of the judiciary, then free discussion and calm appeals to reason and to the justice of the people will not fail to redress the wrong. But until the law shall be declared void by the courts or repealed by Congress no individual or combination of individuals can be justified in forcibly resisting its execution. It is impossible that any government can continue to exist upon any other principles. It would cease to be a government and be unworthy of the name if it had not the power to enforce the execution of its own laws within its own sphere of action.

It is true that cases may be imagined disclosing such a settled purpose of usurpation and oppression on the part of the Government as would justify an appeal to arms. These, however, are extreme cases, which we have no reason to apprehend in a government where the power is in the hands of a patriotic people. And no citizen who loves his country would in any case whatever resort to forcible resistance unless he clearly saw that the time had come when a freeman should prefer death to submission; for if such a struggle is once begun, and the citizens of one section of the country arrayed in arms against those of another in doubtful conflict, let the battle result as it may, there will be an end of the Union and with it an end to the hopes of freedom. The victory of the injured would not secure to them the blessings of liberty; it would avenge their wrongs, but they would themselves share in the common ruin.

But the Constitution cannot be maintained nor the Union preserved, in opposition to public feeling, by the mere exertion of the coercive powers confided to the General Government. The foundations must be laid in the affections of the people, in the security it gives to life, liberty, character, and property in every quarter of the country, and in the fraternal attachment which the citizens of the several States bear to one another as members of one political family, mutually contributing to promote the happiness of each other. Hence the citizens of every State should studiously avoid everything calculated to wound the sensibility or offend the just pride of the people of other States, and they should frown upon any proceedings within their own borders likely to disturb the tranquillity of their political brethren in other portions of the Union. In a country so extensive as the United States, and with pursuits so varied, the internal regulations of the several States must frequently differ from one another in important particulars, and this difference is unavoidably increased by the varying principles upon which the American colonies were originally planted—principles which had taken deep root in their social relations before the Revolution, and therefore of necessity influencing their policy since they became free and independent States. But each State has the unquestionable right to regulate its own internal concerns according to its own pleasure, and while it does not interfere with the rights of the people of other States or the rights of the Union, every State must be the sole judge of the measures proper to secure the safety of its citizens and promote their happiness; and all efforts on the part of people of other States to cast odium upon their institutions, and all measures calculated to disturb their rights of property or to put in jeopardy their peace and internal tranquillity, are in direct opposition to the spirit in which the Union was formed, and must endanger its safety. Motives of philanthropy may be assigned for this unwarrantable interference, and weak men may persuade themselves for a moment that they are laboring in the cause of humanity and asserting the rights of the human race; but everyone, upon sober reflection, will see that nothing but mischief can come from these improper assaults upon the feelings and rights of others. Rest assured that the men found busy in this work of discord are not worthy of your confidence, and deserve your strongest reprobation.

In the legislation of Congress also, and in every measure of the General Government, justice to every portion of the United States should be faithfully observed. No free government can stand without virtue in the people and a lofty spirit of patriotism, and if the sordid feelings of mere selfishness shall usurp the place which ought to be filled by public spirit, the legislation of Congress will soon be converted into a scramble for personal and sectional advantages. Under our free institutions the citizens of every quarter of our country are capable of attaining a high degree of prosperity and happiness without seeking to profit themselves at the expense of others; and every such attempt must in the end fail to succeed, for the people in every part of the United States are too enlightened not to understand their own rights and interests and to detect and defeat every effort to gain undue advantages over them; and when such designs are discovered it naturally provokes resentments which cannot always be easily allayed. Justice—full and ample justice—to every portion of the United States should be the ruling principle of every freeman, and should guide the deliberations of every public body, whether it be State or national.

It is well known that there have always been those amongst us who wish to enlarge the powers of the General Government, and experience would seem to indicate that there is a tendency on the part of this Government to overstep the boundaries marked out for it by the Constitution. Its legitimate authority is abundantly sufficient for all the purposes for which it was created, and its powers being expressly enumerated, there can be no justification for claiming anything beyond them. Every attempt to exercise power beyond these limits should be promptly and firmly opposed, for one evil example will lead to other measures still more mischievous; and if the principle of constructive powers or supposed advantages or temporary circumstances shall ever be permitted to justify the assumption of a power not given by the Constitution, the General Government will before long absorb all the powers of legislation, and you will have in effect but one consolidated government. From the extent of our country, its diversified interests, different pursuits, and different habits, it is too obvious for argument that a single consolidated government would be wholly inadequate to watch over and protect its interests; and every friend of our free institutions should be always prepared to maintain unimpaired and in full vigor the rights and sovereignty of the States and to confine the action of the General Government strictly to the sphere of its appropriate duties.

There is, perhaps, no one of the powers conferred on the Federal Government so liable to abuse as the taxing power. The most productive and convenient sources of revenue were necessarily given to it, that it might be able to perform the important duties imposed upon it; and the taxes which it lays upon commerce being concealed from the real payer in the price of the article, they do not so readily attract the attention of the people as smaller sums demanded from them directly by the taxgatherer. But the tax imposed on goods enhances by so much the price of the commodity to the consumer, and as many of these duties are imposed on articles of necessity which are daily used by the great body of the people, the money raised by these imposts is drawn from their pockets. Congress has no right under the Constitution to take money from the people unless it is required to execute some one of the specific powers entrusted to the Government; and if they raise more than is necessary for such purposes, it is an abuse of the power of taxation, and unjust and oppressive. It may indeed happen that the revenue will sometimes exceed the amount anticipated when the taxes were laid. When, however, this is ascertained it is easy to reduce them, and in such a case it is unquestionably the duty of the Government to reduce them, for no circumstances can justify it in assuming a power not given to it by the Constitution nor in taking away the money of the people when it is not needed for the legitimate wants of the Government.

Plain as these principles appear to be, you will yet find there is a constant effort to induce the General Government to go beyond the limits of its taxing power and to impose unnecessary burdens upon the people. Many powerful interests are continually at work to procure heavy duties on commerce and to swell the revenue beyond the real necessities of the public service, and the country has already felt the injurious effects of their combined influence. They succeeded in obtaining a tariff of duties bearing most oppressively on the agricultural and laboring classes of society and producing a revenue that could not be usefully employed within the range of the powers conferred upon Congress, and in order to fasten upon the people this unjust and unequal system of taxation extravagant schemes of internal improvement were got up in various quarters to squander the money and to purchase support. Thus one unconstitutional measure was intended to be upheld by another, and the abuse of the power of taxation was to be maintained by usurping the power of expending the money in internal improvements. You cannot have forgotten the severe and doubtful struggle through which we passed when the executive department of the Government by its veto endeavored to arrest this prodigal scheme of injustice and to bring back the legislation of Congress to the boundaries prescribed by the Constitution. The good sense and practical judgment of the people when the subject was brought before them sustained the course of the Executive, and this plan of unconstitutional expenditures for the purposes of corrupt influence is, I trust, finally overthrown.

The result of this decision has been felt in the rapid extinguishment of the public debt and the large accumulation of a surplus in the Treasury, notwithstanding the tariff was reduced and is now very far below the amount originally contemplated by its advocates. But, rely upon it, the design to collect an extravagant revenue and to burden you with taxes beyond the economical wants of the Government is not yet abandoned. The various interests which have combined together to impose a heavy tariff and to produce an overflowing Treasury are too strong and have too much at stake to surrender the contest. The corporations and wealthy individuals who are engaged in large manufacturing establishments desire a high tariff to increase their gains. Designing politicians will support it to conciliate their favor and to obtain the means of profuse expenditure for the purpose of purchasing influence in other quarters; and since the people have decided that the Federal Government can not be permitted to employ its income in internal improvements, efforts will be made to seduce and mislead the citizens of the several States by holding out to them the deceitful prospect of benefits to be derived from a surplus revenue collected by the General Government and annually divided among the States; and if, encouraged by these fallacious hopes, the States should disregard the principles of economy which ought to characterize every republican government, and should indulge in lavish expenditures exceeding their resources, they will before long find themselves oppressed with debts which they are unable to pay, and the temptation will become irresistible to support a high tariff in order to obtain a surplus for distribution. Do not allow yourselves, my fellow-citizens, to be misled on this subject. The Federal Government cannot collect a surplus for such purposes without violating the principles of the Constitution and assuming powers which have not been granted. It is, moreover, a system of injustice, and if persisted in will inevitably lead to corrup-

tion, and must end in ruin. The surplus revenue will be drawn from the pockets of the people—from the farmer, the mechanic, and the laboring classes of society; but who will receive it when distributed among the States, where it is to be disposed of by leading State politicians, who have friends to favor and political partisans to gratify? It will certainly not be returned to those who paid it and who have most need of it and are honestly entitled to it. There is but one safe rule, and that is to confine the General Government rigidly within the sphere of its appropriate duties. It has no power to raise a revenue or impose taxes except for the purposes enumerated in the Constitution, and if its income is found to exceed these wants it should be forthwith reduced and the burden of the people so far lightened.

In reviewing the conflicts which have taken place between different interests in the United States and the policy pursued since the adoption of our present form of Government, we find nothing that has produced such deep-seated evil as the course of legislation in relation to the currency. The Constitution of the United States unquestionably intended to secure to the people a circulating medium of gold and silver. But the establishment of a national bank by Congress, with the privilege of issuing paper money receivable in the payment of the public dues, and the unfortunate course of legislation in the several States upon the same subject, drove from general circulation the constitutional currency and substituted one of paper in its place.

It was not easy for men engaged in the ordinary pursuits of business, whose attention had not been particularly drawn to the subject, to foresee all the consequences of a currency exclusively of paper, and we ought not on that account to be surprised at the facility with which laws were obtained to carry into effect the paper system. Honest and even enlightened men are sometimes misled by the specious and plausible statements of the designing. But experience has now proved the mischiefs and dangers of a paper currency, and it rests with you to determine whether the proper remedy shall be applied.

The paper system being founded on public confidence and having of itself no intrinsic value, it is liable to great and sudden fluctuations, thereby rendering property insecure and the wages of labor unsteady and uncertain. The corporations which create the paper money cannot be relied upon to keep the circulating medium uniform in amount. In times of prosperity, when confidence is high, they are tempted by the prospect of gain or by the influence of those who hope to profit by it to extend their issues of paper beyond the bounds of discretion and the reasonable demands of business; and when these issues have been pushed on from day to day, until public confidence is at length shaken, then a reaction takes place, and they immediately withdraw the credits they have given, suddenly curtail their issues, and produce an unexpected and ruinous contraction of the circulating medium, which is felt by the whole community. The banks by this means save themselves, and the mischievous consequences of their imprudence or cupidity are visited upon the public. Nor does the evil stop here. These ebbs and flows in the currency and these indiscreet extensions of credit naturally engender a spirit of speculation injurious to the habits and character of the people. We have already seen its effects in the wild spirit of speculation in the public lands and various kinds of stock which within the last year or two seized upon

such a multitude of our citizens and threatened to pervade all classes of society and to withdraw their attention from the sober pursuits of honest industry. It is not by encouraging this spirit that we shall best preserve public virtue and promote the true interests of our country; but if your currency continues as exclusively paper as it now is, it will foster this eager desire to amass wealth without labor; it will multiply the number of dependents on bank accommodations and bank favors; the temptation to obtain money at any sacrifice will become stronger and stronger, and inevitably lead to corruption, which will find its way into your public councils and destroy at no distant day the purity of your Government. Some of the evils which arise from this system of paper press with peculiar hardship upon the class of society least able to bear it. A portion of this currency frequently becomes depreciated or worthless, and all of it is easily counterfeited in such a manner as to require peculiar skill and much experience to distinguish the counterfeit from the genuine note. These frauds are most generally perpetrated in the smaller notes, which are used in the daily transactions of ordinary business, and the losses occasioned by them are commonly thrown upon the laboring classes of society, whose situation and pursuits put it out of their power to guard themselves from these impositions, and whose daily wages are necessary for their subsistence. It is the duty of every government so to regulate its currency as to protect this numerous class, as far as practicable, from the impositions of avarice and fraud. It is more especially the duty of the United States, where the Government is emphatically the Government of the people, and where this respectable portion of our citizens are so proudly distinguished from the laboring classes of all other nations by their independent spirit, their love of liberty, their intelligence, and their high tone of moral character. Their industry in peace is the source of our wealth and their bravery in war has covered us with glory; and the Government of the United States will but ill discharge its duties if it leaves them a prey to such dishonest impositions. Yet it is evident that their interests cannot be effectually protected unless silver and gold are restored to circulation.

These views alone of the paper currency are sufficient to call for immediate reform; but there is another consideration which should still more strongly press it upon your attention.

Recent events have proved that the paper-money system of this country may be used as an engine to undermine your free institutions, and that those who desire to engross all power in the hands of the few and to govern by corruption or force are aware of its power and prepared to employ it. Your banks now furnish your only circulating medium, and money is plenty or scarce according to the quantity of notes issued by them. While they have capitals not greatly disproportioned to each other, they are competitors in business, and no one of them can exercise dominion over the rest; and although in the present state of the currency these banks may and do operate injuriously upon the habits of business, the pecuniary concerns, and the moral tone of society, yet, from their number and dispersed situation, they cannot combine for the purposes of political influence, and whatever may be the dispositions of some of them, their power of mischief must necessarily be confined to a narrow space and felt only in their immediate neighborhoods.

But when the charter for the Bank of the United States was obtained from Congress it perfected the schemes of the paper system and gave to its advocates the position they have struggled to obtain from the commencement of the Federal Government to the present hour. The immense capital and peculiar privileges bestowed upon it enabled it to exercise despotic sway over the other banks in every part of the country. From its superior strength it could seriously injure, if not destroy, the business of any one of them which might incur its resentment; and it openly claimed for itself the power of regulating the currency throughout the United States. In other words, it asserted (and it undoubtedly possessed) the power to make money plenty or scarce at its pleasure, at any time and in any quarter of the Union, by controlling the issues of other banks and permitting an expansion or compelling a general contraction of the circulating medium, according to its own will. The other banking institutions were sensible of its strength, and they soon generally became its obedient instruments, ready at all times to execute its mandates; and with the banks necessarily went also that numerous class of persons in our commercial cities who depend altogether on bank credits for their solvency and means of business, and who are therefore obliged, for their own safety, to propitiate the favor of the money power by distinguished zeal and devotion in its service. The result of the ill-advised legislation which established this great monopoly was to concentrate the whole moneyed power of the Union, with its boundless means of corruption and its numerous dependents, under the direction and command of one acknowledged head, thus organizing this particular interest as one body and securing to it unity and concert of action throughout the United States, and enabling it to bring forward upon any occasion its entire and undivided strength to support or defeat any measure of the Government. In the hands of this formidable power, thus perfectly organized, was also placed unlimited dominion over the amount of the circulating medium, giving it the power to regulate the value of property and the fruits of labor in every quarter of the Union, and to bestow prosperity or bring ruin upon any city or section of the country as might best comport with its own interest or policy.

We are not left to conjecture how the moneyed power, thus organized and with such a weapon in its hands, would be likely to use it. The distress and alarm which pervaded and agitated the whole country when the Bank of the United States waged war upon the people in order to compel them to submit to its demands cannot yet be forgotten. The ruthless and unsparing temper with which whole cities and communities were oppressed, individuals impoverished and ruined, and a scene of cheerful prosperity suddenly changed into one of gloom and despondency ought to be indelibly impressed on the memory of the people of the United States. If such was its power in a time of peace, what would it not have been in a season of war, with an enemy at your doors? No nation but the freemen of the United States could have come out victorious from such a contest; yet, if you had not conquered, the Government would have passed from the hands of the many to the hands of the few, and this organized money power from its secret conclave would have dictated the choice of your highest officers and compelled you to make peace

or war, as best suited their own wishes. The forms of your Government might for a time have remained, but its living spirit would have departed from it.

The distress and sufferings inflicted on the people by the bank are some of the fruits of that system of policy which is continually striving to enlarge the authority of the Federal Government beyond the limits fixed by the Constitution. The powers enumerated in that instrument do not confer on Congress the right to establish such a corporation as the Bank of the United States, and the evil consequences which followed may warn us of the danger of departing from the true rule of construction and of permitting temporary circumstances or the hope of better promoting the public welfare to influence in any degree our decisions upon the extent of the authority of the General Government. Let us abide by the Constitution as it is written, or amend it in the constitutional mode if it is found to be defective.

The severe lessons of experience will, I doubt not, be sufficient to prevent Congress from again chartering such a monopoly, even if the Constitution did not present an insuperable objection to it. But you must remember, my fellow-citizens, that eternal vigilance by the people is the price of liberty, and that you must pay the price if you wish to secure the blessing. It behooves you, therefore, to be watchful in your States as well as in the Federal Government. The power which the moneyed interest can exercise, when concentrated under a single head and with our present system of currency, was sufficiently demonstrated in the struggle made by the Bank of the United States. Defeated in the General Government, the same class of intriguers and politicians will now resort to the States and endeavor to obtain there the same organization which they failed to perpetuate in the Union; and with specious and deceitful plans of public advantages and State interests and State pride they will endeavor to establish in the different States one moneyed institution with overgrown capital and exclusive privileges sufficient to enable it to control the operations of the other banks. Such an institution will be pregnant with the same evils produced by the Bank of the United States, although its sphere of action is more confined, and in the State in which it is chartered the money power will be able to embody its whole strength and to move together with undivided force to accomplish any object it may wish to attain. You have already had abundant evidence of its power to inflict injury upon the agricultural, mechanical, and laboring classes of society, and over those whose engagements in trade or speculation render them dependent on bank facilities the dominion of the State monopoly will be absolute and their obedience unlimited. With such a bank and a paper currency the money power would in a few years govern the State and control its measures, and if a sufficient number of States can be induced to create such establishments the time will soon come when it will again take the field against the United States and succeed in perfecting and perpetuating its organization by a charter from Congress.

It is one of the serious evils of our present system of banking that it enables one class of society—and that by no means a numerous one—by its control over the currency, to act injuriously upon the interests of all the others and to exercise more than its just proportion of influence in political affairs. The agricultural, the mechanical, and the laboring classes have little or no share in the direction of the great moneyed corporations, and from their habits and the nature of their pursuits they are incapable of forming extensive combinations to act together with united force. Such concert of action may sometimes be produced in a single city or in a small district of country by means of personal communications with each other, but they have no regular or active correspondence with those who are engaged in similar pursuits in distant places; they have but little patronage to give to the press, and exercise but a small share of influence over it; they have no crowd of dependents about them who hope to grow rich without labor by their countenance and favor, and who are therefore always ready to execute their wishes. The planter, the farmer, the mechanic, and the laborer all know that their success depends upon their own industry and economy, and that they must not expect to become suddenly rich by the fruits of their toil. Yet these classes of society form the great body of the people of the United States; they are the bone and sinew of the country—men who love liberty and desire nothing but equal rights and equal laws, and who, moreover, hold the great mass of our national wealth, although it is distributed in moderate amounts among the millions of freemen who possess it. But with overwhelming numbers and wealth on their side they are in constant danger of losing their fair influence in the Government, and with difficulty maintain their just rights against the incessant efforts daily made to encroach upon them. The mischief springs from the power which the moneyed interest derives from a paper currency which they are able to control, from the multitude of corporations with exclusive privileges which they have succeeded in obtaining in the different States, and which are employed altogether for their benefit; and unless you become more watchful in your States and check this spirit of monopoly and thirst for exclusive privileges you will in the end find that the most important powers of Government have been given or bartered away, and the control over your dearest interests has passed into the hands of these corporations.

The paper-money system and its natural associations—monopoly and exclusive privileges—have already struck their roots too deep in the soil, and it will require all your efforts to check its further growth and to eradicate the evil. The men who profit by the abuses and desire to perpetuate them will continue to besiege the halls of legislation in the General Government as well as in the States, and will seek by every artifice to mislead and deceive the public servants. It is to yourselves that you must look for safety and the means of guarding and perpetuating your free institutions. In your hands is rightfully placed the sovereignty of the country, and to you everyone placed in authority is ultimately responsible. It is always in your power to see that the wishes of the people are carried into faithful execution, and their will, when once made known, must sooner or later be obeyed; and while the people remain, as I trust they ever will, uncorrupted and incorruptible, and continue watchful and jealous of their rights, the Government is safe, and the cause of freedom will continue to triumph over all its enemies. . . .

George Bancroft: THE OFFICE OF THE PEOPLE IN ART, GOVERNMENT AND RELIGION

Educated at Harvard and Goettingen, George Bancroft became one of the influential intellectual leaders associated with the Jacksonian party. The first volume of his notable history of the United States was issued in 1834 and, if every page does not actually vote for Jackson, there are many passages which exalt the common man as the source of freedom and happiness in America. The following oration was delivered at Williams College in 1835. It may seem incredible that a scholar trained at Harvard and Goettingen could say that "the decision of the whole is to be preferred to the judgment of the enlightened few" or that "the people collectively are wiser than the most gifted individual," but the reader should give careful attention to Bancroft's attempt to create a transcendental democratic philosophy.

I

THE material world does not change in its masses or in its powers. The stars shine with no more lustre than when they first sang together in the glory of their birth. The flowers that gemmed the fields and the forests, before America was discovered, now bloom around us in their season. The sun that shone on Homer shines on us in unchanging lustre.

From George Bancroft, *Literary and Historical Miscellanies*, New York, 1840, pp. 408–426 abridged.

The bow that beamed on the patriarch still glitters in the clouds. Nature is the same. For her no new forces are generated; no new capacities are discovered. The earth turns on its axis, and perfects its revolutions, and renews its seasons, without increase or advancement.

But a like passive destiny does not attach to the inhabitants of the earth. For them the expectations of social improvement are no delusion; the hopes of philanthropy are more than a dream. The five senses do not constitute the whole inventory of our sources of knowledge. They are the organs by which thought connects itself with the external universe; but the power of thought is not merged in the exercise of its instruments. We have functions which connect us with heaven, as well as organs which set us in relation with earth. We have not merely the senses opening to us the external world, but an internal sense, which places us in connection with the world of intelligence and the decrees of God.

There is a *spirit in man:* not in the privileged few; not in those of us only who by the favor of Providence have been nursed in public schools: IT IS IN MAN: it is the attribute of the race. The spirit, which is the guide to truth, is the gracious gift to each member of the human family.

Reason exists within every breast. I mean not that faculty which deduces inferences from the experience of the senses, but that higher faculty, which from the infinite treasures of its own consciousness originates truth, and assents to it by the force of intuitive evidence; that faculty which raises us beyond the control of time and space, and gives us faith in things eternal and invisible. There is not the difference between one mind and another, which the pride of philosophers might conceive. To them no faculty is

conceded, which does not belong to the meanest of their countrymen. In them there cannot spring up a truth, which does not equally have its germ in every mind. They have not the power of creation; they can but reveal what God has implanted in every breast.

The intellectual functions, by which relations are perceived, are the common endowments of the race. The differences are apparent, not real. The eye in one person may be dull, in another quick, in one distorted, and in another tranquil and clear; yet the relation of the eye to light is in all men the same. Just so judgment may be liable in individual minds to the bias of passion, and yet its relation to truth is immutable, and is universal.

In questions of practical duty, conscience is God's umpire, whose light illumines every heart. There is nothing in books, which had not first, and has not still its life within us. Religion itself is a dead letter, wherever its truths are not renewed in the soul. Individual conscience may be corrupted by interest, or debauched by pride, yet the rule of morality is distinctly marked; its harmonies are to the mind like music to the ear; and the moral judgment, when carefully analyzed and referred to its principles, is always founded in right. The eastern superstition, which bids its victims prostrate themselves before the advancing car of their idols, springs from a noble root, and is but a melancholy perversion of that self-devotion, which enables the Christian to bear the cross, and subject his personal passions to the will of God. Immorality of itself never won to its support the inward voice; conscience, if questioned, never forgets to curse the guilty with the memory of sin, to cheer the upright with the meek tranquillity of approval. And this admirable power, which is the instinct of Deity, is the attribute of every man; it knocks at the palace gate, it dwells in the meanest hovel. Duty, like death, enters every abode, and delivers its message. Conscience, like reason and judgment, is universal.

That the moral affections are planted everywhere, needs only to be asserted to be received. The savage mother loves her offspring with all the fondness that a mother can know. Beneath the odorous shade of the boundless forests of Chili, the native youth repeats the story of love as sincerely as it was ever chanted in the valley of Vaucluse. The affections of family are not the growth of civilization. The charities of life are scattered everywhere; enamelling the vales of human being, as the flowers paint the meadows. They are not the fruit of study, nor the privilege of refinement, but a natural instinct.

Our age has seen a revolution in works of imagination. The poet has sought his theme in common life. Never is the genius of Scott more pathetic, than when, as in *The Antiquary,* he delineates the sorrows of a poor fisherman, or as in *The Heart of Midlothian,* he takes the heroine from a cottage. And even Wordsworth, the purest and most original poet of the day, in spite of the inveterate character of his political predilections, has thrown the light of genius on the walks of commonest life; he finds a lesson in every grave of the village churchyard; he discloses the boundless treasures of feeling in the peasant, the laborer and the artisan; the strolling peddler becomes, through his genius, a teacher of the sublimest morality; and the solitary wagoner, the lonely shepherd, even the feeble mother of an idiot boy, furnishes lessons in the reverence for Humanity.

If from things relating to truth, justice, and affection, we turn to those relating to the beautiful, we may here still further assert, that the sentiment for the beautiful resides in every breast. The lovely forms of the external world delight us from their adaptation to our powers.

Yea, what were mighty Nature's self?
  Her features could they win us,
Unhelped by the poetic voice
  That hourly speaks within us?

The Indian mother, on the borders of Hudson's Bay, decorates her manufactures with ingenious devices and lovely colors, prompted by the same instinct which guided the pencil and mixed the colors of Raphael. The inhabitant of Nootka Sound tattoos his body with the method of harmonious Arabesques. Every form, to which the hands of the artist have ever given birth, sprung first into being as a conception of his mind, from a natural faculty, which belongs not to the artist exclusively, but to man. Beauty, like truth and justice, lives within us; like virtue and like moral law, it is a companion of the soul. The power which leads to the production of beautiful forms, or to the perception of them in the works which God has made, is an attribute of Humanity....

II

If it be true, that the gifts of mind and heart are universally diffused, if the sentiment of truth, justice, love, and beauty exists in every one, then it follows, as a necessary consequence, that the common judgment in taste, politics, and religion, is the highest authority on earth, and the nearest possible approach to an infallible decision. From the consideration of individual powers I turn to the action of the human mind in masses.

If reason is a universal faculty, the universal decision is the nearest criterion of truth. The common mind winnows opinions; it is the sieve which separates error from certainty. The exercise by many of the same faculty on the same subject would naturally lead to the same conclusions. But if not, the very differences of opinion that arise prove the supreme judgment of the general mind. Truth is one. It never contradicts itself. One truth cannot contradict another truth. Hence truth is a bond of union. But error not only contradicts truth, but may contradict itself; so that there may be many errors, and each at variance with the rest. Truth is therefore of necessity an element of harmony; error as necessarily an element of discord. Thus there can be no continuing universal judgment but a right one. Men cannot agree in an absurdity; neither can they agree in a falsehood.

If wrong opinions have often been cherished by the masses, the cause always lies in the complexity of the ideas presented. Error finds its way into the soul of a nation, only through the channel of truth. It is to a truth that men listen; and if they accept error also, it is only because the error is for the time so closely interwoven with the truth, that the one cannot readily be separated from the other. . . .

III

In like manner the best government rests on the people and not on the few, on persons and not on property, on the free development of public opinion and not on authority; because the munificent Author of our being has conferred the gifts of mind upon every member of the human race without distinction of outward circumstances. Whatever of other possessions may be engrossed, mind asserts its own independence. Lands, estates, the produce of mines, the prolific abundance of the seas, may be usurped by a privileged class. Avarice, assuming the form of ambitious power, may grasp realm after realm, subdue continents, compass the earth in its schemes of aggrandizement, and sigh after other worlds; but mind eludes the power of appropriation; it exists only in its own individuality; it is a property which cannot be confiscated and cannot be torn away; it laughs at chains; it bursts from imprisonment; it defies monopoly. A government of equal rights must, therefore, rest upon mind; not wealth, not brute force, the sum of the moral intelligence of the community should rule the State. Prescription can no more assume to be a valid plea for political injustice; society studies to eradicate established abuses, and to bring social institutions and laws into harmony with moral right; not dismayed by the natural and necessary imperfections of all human effort, and not giving way to despair, because every hope does not at once ripen into fruit.

The public happiness is the true object of legislation, and can be secured only by the masses of mankind themselves awakening to the knowledge and the care of their own interests. Our free institutions have reversed the false and ignoble distinctions between men; and refusing to gratify the pride of caste, have acknowledged the common mind to be the true material for a commonwealth. Everything has hitherto been done for the happy few. It is not possible to endow an aristocracy with greater benefits than they have already enjoyed; there is no room to hope that individuals will be more highly gifted or more fully developed than the greatest sages of past times. The world can advance only through the culture of the moral and intellectual powers of the people. To accomplish this end by means of the people themselves, is the highest purpose of government. If it be the duty of the individual to strive after a perfection like the perfection of God, how much more ought a nation to be the image of Deity. The common mind is the true Parian marble, fit to be wrought into likeness to a God. The duty of America is to secure the culture and the happiness of the masses by their reliance on themselves.

The absence of the prejudices of the old world leaves us here the opportunity of consulting independent truth; and man is left to apply the instinct of freedom to every social relation and public interest. We have approached so near to nature, that we can hear her gentlest whispers; we have made Humanity our lawgiver and our oracle; and, therefore, the nation receives, vivifies and applies principles, which in Europe the wisest accept with distrust. Freedom of mind and of conscience, freedom of the seas, freedom of industry, equality of franchises, each great truth is firmly grasped, comprehended, and enforced; for the multitude is neither rash nor fickle. In truth, it is less fickle than those who profess to be its guides. Its natural dialectics surpass the logic of the schools. Political action has never been so consistent and so unwavering, as when it results from a feeling or a principle, diffused through society. The people is firm and tranquil in its movements, and necessarily acts with moderation, because it becomes but slowly impregnated with new ideas; and effects no changes, except in harmony with the knowledge which it has acquired. Besides, where it is permanently possessed of power, there exists neither the occasion nor the desire for frequent change. It is not the parent of tumult; sedition is bred in the lap of luxury, and its chosen emissaries are the beggared spendthrift and the impoverished libertine. The government by the people is

in very truth the strongest government in the world. Discarding the implements of terror, it dares to rule by moral force, and has its citadel in the heart.

Such is the political system which rests on reason, reflection, and the free expression of deliberate choice. There may be those who scoff at the suggestion, that the decision of the whole is to be preferred to the judgment of the enlightened few. They say in their hearts that the masses are ignorant; that farmers know nothing of legislation; that mechanics should not quit their workshops to join in forming public opinion. But true political science does indeed venerate the masses. It maintains, not as has been perversely asserted, that "the people can make right," but that the people can DISCERN right. Individuals are but shadows, too often engrossed by the pursuit of shadows; the race is immortal: individuals are of limited sagacity; the common mind is infinite in its experience: individuals are languid and blind; the many are ever wakeful: individuals are corrupt; the race has been redeemed: individuals are time-serving; the masses are fearless: individuals may be false, the masses are ingenuous and sincere: individuals claim the divine sanction of truth for the deceitful conceptions of their own fancies; the Spirit of God breathes through the combined intelligence of the people. Truth is not to be ascertained by the impulses of an individual; it emerges from the contradictions of personal opinions; it raises itself in majestic serenity above the strifes of parties and the conflict of sects; it acknowledges neither the solitary mind, nor the separate faction as its oracle; but owns as its only faithful interpreter the dictates of pure reason itself, proclaimed by the general voice of mankind. The decrees of the universal conscience are the nearest approach to the presence of God in the soul of man.

Thus the opinion which we respect is, indeed, not the opinion of one or of a few, but the sagacity of the many. It is hard for the pride of cultivated philosophy to put its ear to the ground, and listen reverently to the voice of lowly humanity; yet the people collectively are wiser than the most gifted individual, for all his wisdom constitutes but a part of theirs. When the great sculptor of Greece was endeavoring to fashion the perfect model of beauty, he did not passively imitate the form of the loveliest woman of his age; but he gleaned the several lineaments of his faultless work from the many. And so it is, that a perfect judgment is the result of comparison, when error eliminates error, and truth is established by concurring witnesses. The organ of truth is the invisible decision of the unbiased world; she pleads before no tribunal but public opinion; she owns no safe interpreter but the common mind; she knows no court of appeals but the soul of humanity. It is when the multitude give counsel, that right purposes find safety; theirs is the fixedness that cannot be shaken; theirs is the understanding which exceeds in wisdom; theirs is the heart, of which the largeness is as the sand on the seashore.

It is not by vast armies, by immense natural resources, by accumulations of treasure, that the greatest results in modern civilization have been accomplished. The traces of the career of conquest pass away, hardly leaving a scar on the national intelligence. The famous battle-grounds of victory are, most of them, comparatively indifferent to the human race; barren fields of blood, the scourges of their times, but affecting the social condition as little as the raging of a pestilence. Not one benevolent institution, not one ameliorating principle in the Roman state, was a voluntary concession of the aristocracy; each useful element was borrowed from the Democracies of Greece, or was a reluctant concession to the demands of the people. The same is true in modern political life. It is the confession of an enemy to Democracy, that "ALL THE GREAT AND NOBLE INSTITUTIONS OF THE WORLD HAVE COME FROM POPULAR EFFORTS." . . .

The Democratic Review: THE DEMOCRATIC PRINCIPLE

In 1837, a group of Jacksonian writers conceived the idea of establishing a Democratic literary magazine. Andrew Jackson and other Democratic leaders encouraged the project and the United States Magazine and Democratic Review *was launched in October of that year. John L. O'Sullivan, the flamboyant editor, quickly made the new journal a vigorous formulator of Democratic opinion and taste in politics, literature, and the arts. The selection which follows is the opening editorial in the first number of the* Democratic Review *and can be taken as a codification of the democratic ideas held by the followers of Jackson. Although there are some differences which reflect the social experience of the Jacksonians, much of the editorial seems to be little more than a reiteration of Jeffersonian principles.*

SO many false ideas have insensibly attached themselves to the term "democracy," as connected with our party politics, that we deem it necessary here, at the outset, to make a full and free profession of the cardinal principles of political faith on which we take our stand; principles to which we are devoted with an unwavering force of conviction and earnestness of enthusiasm which, ever since they were first presented to our minds, have constantly grown and strengthened by contemplation of them, and of the incalculable capabilities of social improvement of which they contain the germs.

We believe, then, in the principle of *democratic republicanism*, in its strongest and purest sense. We have an abiding confidence in the virtue, intelligence, and full capacity for self-government, of the great mass of our people—our industrious, honest, manly, intelligent millions of freemen.

We are opposed to all self-styled "wholesome restraints" on the free action of the popular opinion and will, other than those which have for their sole object the prevention of precipitate legislation. This latter object is to be attained by the expedient of the division of power, and by causing all legislation to pass through the ordeal of successive forms; to be sifted through the discussions of co-ordinate legislative branches, with mutual suspensive veto powers. Yet all should be dependent with equal directness and promptness on the influence of public opinion; the popular will should be equally the animating and moving spirit of them all, and ought never to find in any of its own creatures a self-imposed power, capable (when misused either by corrupt ambition or honest error) of resisting itself, and defeating its own determined object. We cannot, therefore, look with an eye of favor on any such forms of representation as, by length of tenure of delegated power, tend to weaken that universal and unrelaxing responsibility to the vigilance of public opinion, which is the true conservative principle of our institutions.

The great question here occurs, which

is of vast importance to this country (was it not once near dissolving the Union, and plunging it into the abyss of civil war?), of the relative rights of majorities and minorities. Though we go for the republican principle of the supremacy of the will of the majority, we acknowledge, in general, a strong sympathy with minorities, and consider that their rights have a high moral claim on the respect and justice of majorities; a claim not always fairly recognized in practice by the latter, in the full sway of power, when flushed with triumph, and impelled by strong interests. This has ever been the point of the democratic cause most open to assault, and most difficult to defend. This difficulty does not arise from any intrinsic weakness. The democratic theory is perfect and harmonious in all its parts; and if this point is not so self-evidently clear as the rest is generally, in all candid discussion, conceded to be, it is because of certain false principles of government, which have, in all practical experiments of the theory, been interwoven with the democratic portions of the system, being borrowed from the example of anti-democratic systems of government. We shall always be willing to meet this question frankly and fairly. The great argument against pure democracy, drawn from this source, is this:

Though the main object with reference to which all social institutions ought to be modelled is undeniably, as stated by the democrat, "the greatest good of the greatest number," yet it by no means follows that the greatest number always rightly understands its own greatest good. Highly pernicious error has often possessed the minds of nearly a whole nation; while the philosopher in his closet, and an enlightened few about him, powerless against the overwhelming current of popular prejudice and excitement, have alone possessed the truth, which the next generation may perhaps recognize and practice, though its author, now sainted, has probably, in his own time, been its martyr. The original adoption of the truth would have saved perhaps oceans of blood, and mountains of misery and crime. How much stronger, then, the case against the absolute supremacy of the opinion and will of the majority, when its numerical preponderance is, as often happens, comparatively small. And if the larger proportion of the more wealthy and cultivated classes of the society are found on the side of the minority, the disinterested observer may well be excused if he hesitate long before he awards the judgment, in a difficult and complicated question, in favor of the mere numerical argument. Majorities are often as liable to error of opinion, and not always free from a similar proneness to selfish abuse of power, as minorities; and a vast amount of injustice may often be perpetrated, and consequent general social injury be done, before the evil reaches that extreme at which it rights itself by revolution, moral or physical.

We have here, we believe, correctly stated the anti-democratic side of the argument on this point. It is not to be denied that it possesses something more than plausibility. It has certainly been the instrument of more injury to the cause of the democratic principle than all the bayonets and cannon that have ever been arrayed in support of it against the principle. The inference from it is, that the popular opinion and will must not be trusted with the supreme and absolute direction of the general interests; that it must be subjected to the "conservative checks" of minority interests, and to the regulation of the "more enlightened wisdom" of the "better classes," and those to whom the possession of a property "test of merit" gives what they term "a stake in the community." And here we find ourselves in the face of the great stronghold of the anti-democratic, or *aristocratic,* principle.

It is not our purpose, in this place, to carry out the discussion of this question. The general scope and tendency of the present work are designed to be directed towards the refutation of this sophistical reasoning and inference. It will be sufficient here to allude to the leading ideas by which they are met by the advocate of the pure democratic cause.

In the first place, the greatest number are *more likely,* at least, as a general rule, to understand and follow their own greatest good, than is the minority.

In the second, a minority is much more likely to abuse power for the promotion of its own selfish interests, at the expense of the majority of numbers—the substantial and producing mass of the nation—than the latter is to oppress unjustly the former. The social evil is also, in that case, proportionately greater. This is abundantly proved by the history of all aristocratic interests that have existed, in various degrees and modifications, in the world. A majority cannot subsist upon a minority; while the natural, and in fact uniform, tendency of a minority entrusted with governmental authority is, to surround itself with wealth, splendor, and power, at the expense of the producing mass, creating and perpetuating those artificial social distinctions which violate the natural equality of rights of the human race, and at the same time offend and degrade the true dignity of human nature.

In the third place, there does not naturally exist any such original superiority of a minority class above the great mass of a community, in intelligence and competence for the duties of government—even putting out of view its constant tendency to abuse from selfish motives, and the safer honesty of the mass. The general diffusion of education; the facility of access to every species of knowledge important to the great interests of the community; the freedom of the press, whose very licentiousness cannot materially impair its permanent value, in this country at least, make the pretensions of those self-styled "better classes" to the sole possession of the requisite intelligence for the management of public affairs, too absurd to be entitled to any other treatment than an honest, manly contempt. As far as superior knowledge and talent confer on their possessor a natural charter of privilege to control his associates, and exert an influence on the direction of the general affairs of the community, the free and natural action of that privilege is best secured by a perfectly free democratic system, which will abolish all artificial distinctions, and, preventing the accumulation of any social obstacles to advancement, will permit the free development of every germ of talent, wherever it may chance to exist, whether on the proud mountain summit, in the humble valley, or by the wayside of common life.

But the question is not yet satisfactorily answered, how the relation between majorities and minorities, in the frequent case of a collision of sentiments and particular interests, is to be so adjusted as to secure a mutual respect of rights, to preserve harmony and good will, and save society from the *malum extremum discordia,* from being as a house divided against itself—and thus to afford free scope to that competition, discussion, and mutual moral influence, which cannot but result, in the end, in the ascendency of the truth, and in "the greatest good of the greatest number." On the one side, it has only been shown that the absolute government of the majority does not always afford a perfect guarantee against the misuse of its numerical power over the weakness of the minority. On the other, it has been shown that this chance of misuse is, as a general rule, far less than in the opposite relation of the ascendency of a minority; and that the evils attendant upon it are infinitely less, in every point of view, in the one case than the other. But this is not yet a complete or satisfactory solution of the problem. Have we but a choice of evils? Is there, then, such a radical deficiency in the moral elements implanted by its Creator in human society, that no other alternative can be devised by which both evils shall be avoided, and a result attained more analogous to the beautiful and glorious harmony of the rest of his creation?

It were scarcely consistent with a true and living faith in the existence and attributes of that Creator, so to believe; and such is not the democratic belief. The reason of the plausibility with which appeal may be made to the experience of so many republics, to sustain this argument against democratic institutions, is, that the true theory of national self-government has been hitherto but imperfectly understood; bad principles have been mixed up with the good; and the republican government has been administered on ideas and in a spirit borrowed from the strong governments of the other forms; and to the corruptions and manifold evils which have never failed, in the course of time, to evolve themselves out of these seeds of destruction, is ascribable the eventual failure of those experiments, and the consequent doubt and discredit which have attached themselves to the democratic principles on which they were, in the outset, mainly based.

It is under the word *government,* that the subtle danger lurks. Understood as a central consolidated power, managing and directing the various general interests of the society, all government is evil, and the parent of evil. A strong and active democratic *government,* in the common sense of the term, is an evil, differing only in degree and mode of operation, and not in nature, from a strong despotism. This difference is certainly vast, yet, inasmuch as these strong governmental powers must be wielded by human agents, even as the powers of the despotism, it is, after all, only a difference in degree; and the tendency to demoralization and tyranny is the same, though the development of the evil results is much more gradual and slow in the one case than in the other. Hence the demagogue—hence the faction—hence the mob—hence the violence, licentiousness, and instability—hence the ambitious struggles of parties and their leaders for power—hence the abuses of that power by majorities and their leaders—hence the indirect oppressions of the general by partial interests—hence (fearful symptom) the demoralization of the great men of the nation, and of the nation itself, proceeding (unless checked in time by the more healthy and patriotic portion of the mind of the nation rallying itself to reform the principles and sources of the evil) gradually to that point of maturity at which relief from the tumult of moral and physical confusion is to be found only under the shelter of an energetic armed despotism.

The best government is that which governs least. No human depositories can, with safety, be trusted with the power of legislation upon the general interests of society so as to operate directly or indirectly on the industry and property of the community. Such power must be perpetually liable to the most pernicious abuse, from the natural imperfection, both in wisdom of judgment and purity of purpose, of all human legislation, exposed constantly to the pressure of partial interests; interests which, at the same time that they are essentially selfish and tyrannical, are ever vigilant, persevering, and subtle in all the arts of deception and corruption. In fact, the whole history of human society and government may be safely appealed to, in evidence that the abuse of such power a thousandfold more than overbalances its beneficial use. Legislation has been the fruitful parent of nine-tenths of all the evil, moral and physical, by which mankind has been afflicted since the creation of the world, and by which human nature has been self-degraded, fettered, and oppressed. Government should have as little as possible to do with the general business and interests of the people. If it once undertake these functions as its rightful province of action, it is impossible to say to it "thus far shalt thou go, and no farther." It will be impossible to confine it to the public interests of the *commonwealth.* It will be perpetually tampering with private interests, and sending forth seeds of corruption which will result in the demoralization of the society. Its domestic action should be confined to the administration of justice, for the protection of the natural equal rights of the citizen, and the preservation of social order. In all other respects, the VOLUNTARY PRINCIPLE, the principle of FREEDOM, suggested to us by the analogy of the divine government of the Creator, and already recognized by us with perfect success in the great social

interest of Religion, affords the true "golden rule" which is alone abundantly competent to work out the best possible general result of order and happiness from that chaos of characters, ideas, motives, and interests—human society. Afford but the single nucleus of a system of administration of justice between man and man, and, under the sure operation of this principle, the floating atoms will distribute and combine themselves, as we see in the beautiful natural process of crystallization, into a far more perfect and harmonious result than if government, with its "fostering hand," undertake to disturb, under the plea of directing, the process. The natural laws which will establish themselves and find their own level are the best laws. The same hand was the Author of the moral, as of the physical world; and we feel clear and strong in the assurance that we cannot err in trusting, in the former, to the same fundamental principles of spontaneous action and self-regulation which produce the beautiful order of the latter. . . .

This is all generalization, and therefore, though necessary, probably dull. We have endeavored to state the theory of the Jeffersonian democracy, to which we profess allegiance, in its abstract essence, however unpopular it appears to be, in these latter days, to "theorize." These are the original ideas of American democracy; and we would not give much for that "practical knowledge" which is ignorant of, and affects to disregard, the essential and abstract principles which really constitute the animating soul of what were else lifeless and naught. The application of these ideas to practice, in our political affairs, is obvious and simple. Penetrated with a perfect faith in their eternal truth, we can never hesitate as to the direction to which, in every practical case arising, they must point with the certainty of the magnetized needle; and we have no desire to shrink from the responsibility, at the outset, of a frank avowal of them in the broadest general language.

But having done so, we will not be further misunderstood, and we hope not misrepresented, as to immediate practical views. We deem it scarcely necessary to say that we are opposed to all precipitate radical changes in social institutions. Adopting "Nature as the best guide," we cannot disregard the lesson which she teaches, when she accomplishes her most mighty results of the good and beautiful by the silent and slow operation of great principles, without the convulsions of too rapid action. *Festina lente* is an invaluable precept, if it be not abused. On the other hand, that specious sophistry ought to be no less watchfully guarded against, by which old evils always struggle to perpetuate themselves by appealing to our veneration for "the wisdom of our fathers," to our inert love of present tranquillity, and our natural apprehension of possible danger from the untried and unknown—

> Better to bear the present ills we know,
> Than fly to others that we know not of.

We are not afraid of that much dreaded phrase, "untried experiment," which looms so fearfully before the eyes of some of our most worthy and valued friends. The whole history of the progress hitherto made by humanity, in every respect of social amelioration, records but a series of *"experiments."* The American revolution was the greatest of "experiments," and one of which it is not easy at this day to appreciate the gigantic boldness. Every step in the onward march of improvement by the human race is an "experiment"; and the present

is most emphatically an age of "experiments." The eye of man looks naturally *forward;* and as he is carried onward by the progress of time and truth, he is far more likely to stumble and stray if he turn his face backward, and keep his looks fixed on the thoughts and things of the past. We feel safe under the banner of the democratic principle, which is borne onward by an unseen hand of Providence, to lead our race toward the high destinies of which every human soul contains the God-implanted germ; and of the advent of which—certain, however distant—a dim prophetic presentiment has existed, in one form or another, among all nations in all ages. We are willing to make every reform in our institutions that may be commanded by the test of the democratic principle—to *democratize* them—but only so rapidly as shall appear, to the most cautious wisdom, consistent with a due regard to the existing development of public opinion and to the permanence of the progress made. Every instance in which the action of *government* can be simplified, and one of the hundred giant arms curtailed, with which it now stretches around its fatal protecting grasp over almost all the various interests of society, to substitute the truly healthful action of the free voluntary principle—every instance in which the operation of the public opinion and will, fairly signified, can be brought to bear more directly upon the action of delegated powers—we would regard as so much gained for the true interest of the society and of mankind at large. In this path we cannot go wrong; it is only necessary to be cautious not to go too fast.

Such is, then, our democracy. It of course places us in the school of the strictest construction of the constitution; and in that appears to be involved a full committal of opinion on all the great po- litical questions which now agitate the public mind, and to which we deem it unnecessary here to advert in detail. One necessary inference from the views ex- pressed above is, that we consider the preservation of the present ascendency of the democratic party as of great, if not vital, importance to the future des- tinies of this holy cause. Most of its lead- ing members we know to possess all the qualifications that should entitle men to the confidence and attachment of their country; and the arduous functions of the executive department of the govern- ment are administered with an efficiency, and a strictness and purity of principle, which, considering their nature, extent, and complexity, are indeed remarkable. And even without a particular knowl- edge of the men, the principle alone would still of necessity attach us to that party. The acquisition of the vast influ- ence of the executive department by the present Opposition principles, we could not look upon but as a staggering blow to the cause of democracy, and all the high interests committed with it; from which it would take a long and indefi- nite period of years to recover—even if the loss of time in national progress would not, in that event, have to be reckoned by generations! We shall there- fore, while devoting ourselves to pre- serve and improve the purity of our dem- ocratic institutions, labor to sustain the present democratic administration, by fair appeal to argument, with all the earnestness due to the gravity of the principles and interests involved. . . .

Orestes Brownson: THE LABORING CLASSES

Orestes Brownson was one of the restless reformers of the Jacksonian generation. He had been successively a Presbyterian, a Universalist, and an agnostic before reaching a temporary accommodation with Unitari- anism in the late 1830's. Earlier in the decade, he had been associated with the New York Workingmen's Party, but, by 1838, he had become editor of the Boston Quarterly Review *and a vigorous advocate of the ideas of the radical, Loco-Foco, wing of the Democratic party. The selection which follows appeared in the* Boston Quarterly Review *in July, 1840. In it, Brownson sets forth a startling vision of class warfare between the propertyless workers and the middle classes. Yet, his pro- posed remedy does not seem to depart from the middle-class ideal of individual competition.*

NO one can observe the signs of the times with much care, without per- ceiving that a crisis as to the relation of wealth and labor is approaching. It is useless to shut our eyes to the fact, and like the ostrich fancy ourselves secure be- cause we have so concealed our heads that we see not the danger. We or our children will have to meet this crisis. The old war between the King and the Bar-

ons is well nigh ended, and so is that between the Barons and the Merchants and
Manufacturers—landed capital and commercial capital. The business man has become the peer of my Lord. And now
commences the new struggle between
the operative and his employer, between
wealth and labor. Every day does this
struggle extend further and wax stronger
and fiercer; what or when the end will
be God only knows.

In this coming contest there is a deeper
question at issue than is commonly imagined; a question which is but remotely
touched in your controversies about
United States Banks and Sub Treasuries,
chartered Banking and free Banking,
free trade and corporations, although
these controversies may be paving the
way for it to come up. We have discovered no presentiment of it in any king's
or queen's speech, nor in any president's
message. It is embraced in no popular
political creed of the day, whether chris-
tened Whig or Tory, *Juste-milieu* or
Democratic. No popular senator, or dep-
uty, or peer seems to have any glimpse
of it; but it is working in the hearts of
the million, is struggling to shape itself,
and one day it will be uttered, and in
thunder tones. Well will it be for him,
who, on that day, shall be found ready
to answer it.

What we would ask is, throughout the
Christian world, the actual condition of
the laboring classes, viewed simply and
exclusively in their capacity of laborers?
They constitute at least a moiety of the
human race. We exclude the nobility, we
exclude also the middle class, and include only actual laborers, who are laborers and not proprietors, owners of
none of the funds of production, neither
houses, shops, nor lands, nor implements
of labor, being therefore solely dependent on their hands. We have no means

of ascertaining their precise proportion to
the whole number of the race; but we
think we may estimate them at one half.
In any contest they will be as two to one,
because the large class of proprietors who
are not employers, but laborers on their
own lands or in their own shops will
make common cause with them.

Now we will not so belie our acquaintance with political economy, as to
allege that these alone perform all that is
necessary to the production of wealth.
We are not ignorant of the fact, that the
merchant, who is literally the common
carrier and exchange dealer, performs a
useful service, and is therefore entitled
to a portion of the proceeds of labor. But
make all necessary deductions on his account, and then ask what portion of the
remainder is retained, either in kind or
in its equivalent, in the hands of the
original producer, the workingman? All
over the world this fact stares us in the
face, the workingman is poor and de-
pressed, while a large portion of the non-
workingmen, in the sense we now use
the term, are wealthy. It may be laid
down as a general rule, with but few exceptions, that men are rewarded in an
inverse ratio to the amount of actual
service they perform. Under every government on earth the largest salaries are
annexed to those offices, which demand
of their incumbents the least amount of
actual labor either mental or manual.
And this is in perfect harmony with the
whole system of repartition of the fruits
of industry, which obtains in every department of society. Now here is the system which prevails, and here is its result. The whole class of simple laborers
are poor, and in general unable to procure anything beyond the bare necessaries of life.

In regard to labor two systems obtain;
one that of slave labor, the other that of

free labor. Of the two, the first is, in our judgment, except so far as the feelings are concerned, decidedly the least oppressive. If the slave has never been a free man, we think, as a general rule, his sufferings are less than those of the free laborer at wages. As to actual freedom one has just about as much as the other. The laborer at wages has all the disadvantages of freedom and none of its blessings, while the slave, if denied the blessings, is freed from the disadvantages. We are no advocates of slavery, we are as heartily opposed to it as any modern abolitionist can be; but we say frankly that, if there must always be a laboring population distinct from proprietors and employers, we regard the slave system as decidedly preferable to the system at wages. It is no pleasant thing to go days without food, to lie idle for weeks, seeking work and finding none, to rise in the morning with a wife and children you love, and know not where to procure them a breakfast, and to see constantly before you no brighter prospect than the almshouse. Yet these are no unfrequent incidents in the lives of our laboring population. Even in seasons of general prosperity, when there was only the ordinary cry of "hard times," we have seen hundreds of people in a no very populous village, in a wealthy portion of our common country, suffering for the want of the necessaries of life, willing to work, and yet finding no work to do. Many and many is the application of a poor man for work, merely for his food, we have seen rejected. These things are little thought of, for the applicants are poor; they fill no conspicuous place in society, and they have no biographers. But their wrongs are chronicled in heaven. It is said there is no want in this country. There may be less than in some other countries. But death by actual starvation in this country is, we apprehend, no uncommon occurrence. The sufferings of a quiet, unassuming but useful class of females in our cities, in general seamstresses, too proud to beg or to apply to the almshouse, are not easily told. They are industrious; they do all that they can find to do; but yet the little there is for them to do, and the miserable pittance they receive for it, is hardly sufficient to keep soul and body together. And yet there is a man who employs them to make shirts, trousers, & c., and grows rich on their labors. He is one of our respectable citizens, perhaps is praised in the newspapers for his liberal donations to some charitable institution. He passes among us as a pattern of morality, and is honored as a worthy Christian. And why should he not be, since our *Christian* community is made up of such as he, and since our clergy would not dare question his piety, lest they should incur the reproach of infidelity, and lose their standing, and their salaries? Nay, since our clergy are raised up, educated, fashioned, and sustained by such as he? Not a few of our churches rest on Mammon for their foundation. The basement is a trader's shop.

We pass through our manufacturing villages, most of them appear neat and flourishing. The operatives are well-dressed, and we are told, well paid. They are said to be healthy, contented, and happy. This is the fair side of the picture; the side exhibited to distinguished visitors. There is a dark side, moral as well as physical. Of the common operatives, few, if any, by their wages, acquire a competence. A few of what Carlyle terms not inaptly the *body-servants* are well paid, and now and then an agent or an overseer rides in his coach. But the great mass wear out their health, spirits, and morals, without becoming one whit better off than when they commenced labor. The bills of mortality in these factory villages are not striking, we admit, for the poor girls when they can toil no longer go home to die. The average life, working life we mean, of the girls that come to Lowell, for instance, from Maine, New Hampshire, and Vermont, we have been assured, is only about three years. What becomes of them then? Few of them ever marry; fewer still ever return to their native places with reputations unimpaired. "She has worked in a Factory," is almost enough to damn to infamy the most worthy and virtuous girl. We know no sadder sight on earth than one of our factory villages presents, when the bell at break of day, or at the hour of breakfast, or dinner, calls out its hundreds or thousands of operatives. We stand and look at these hard-working men and women hurrying in all directions, and ask ourselves, where go the proceeds of their labors? The man who employs them, and for whom they are toiling as so many slaves, is one of our city nabobs, revelling in luxury; or he is a member of our legislature, enacting laws to put money in his own pocket; or he is a member of Congress, contending for a high Tariff to tax the poor for the benefit of the rich; or in these times he is shedding crocodile tears over the deplorable condition of the poor laborer, while he docks his wages twenty-five per cent; building miniature log cabins, shouting Harrison and "hard cider." And this man too would fain pass for a Christian and a republican. He shouts for liberty, stickles for equality, and is horrified at a Southern planter who keeps slaves.

One thing is certain; that of the amount actually produced by the operative, he retains a less proportion than it costs the master to feed, clothe, and lodge his slave. Wages is a cunning device of the devil, for the benefit of tender consciences, who would retain all the advantages of the slave system, without the expense, trouble, and odium of being slave-holders.

Messrs. Thome and Kimball, in their account of emancipation in the West Indies, establish the fact that the employer may have the same amount of labor done, twenty-five per cent cheaper than the master. What does this fact prove, if not that wages is a more successful method of taxing labor than slavery? We really believe our Northern system of labor is more oppressive, and even more mischievous to morals, than the Southern. We, however, war against both. We have no toleration for either system. We would see the slave a man, but a free man, not a mere operative at wages. This he would not be were he now emancipated. Could the abolitionists effect all they propose, they would do the slave no service. Should emancipation work as well as they say, still it would do the slave no good. He would be a slave still, although with the title and cares of a freeman. If then we had no constitutional objections to abolitionism, we could not, for the reason here implied, be abolitionists.

The slave system, however, in name and form, is gradually disappearing from Christendom. It will not subsist much longer. But its place is taken by the system of labor at wages, and this system, we hold, is no improvement upon the one it supplants. Nevertheless the system of wages will triumph. It is the system which in name sounds honester than slavery, and in substance is more profitable to the master. It yields the wages of iniquity, without its opprobrium. It will therefore supplant slavery, and be sustained—for a time.

Now, what is the prospect of those who fall under the operation of this system? We ask, is there a reasonable chance that any considerable portion of the present generation of laborers, shall ever become owners of a sufficient portion of the funds of production, to be able to sustain themselves by laboring on their own capital, that is, as independent laborers? We need not ask this question, for everybody knows there is not. Well, is the condition of a laborer at wages the best that the great mass of the working people ought to be able to aspire to? Is it a condition—nay can it be made a condition—with which a man should be satisfied; in which he should be contented to live and die?

In our own country this condition has existed under its most favorable aspects, and has been made as good as it can be. It has reached all the excellence of which it is susceptible. It is now not improving but growing worse. The actual condition of the workingman today, viewed in all its bearings, is not so good as it was fifty years ago. If we have not been altogether misinformed, fifty years ago, health and industrious habits, constituted no mean stock in trade, and with them almost any man might aspire to competence and independence. But it is so no longer. The wilderness has receded, and already the new lands are beyond the reach of the mere laborer, and the employer has him at his mercy. If the present relation subsist, we see nothing better for him in reserve than what he now possesses, but something altogether worse.

We are not ignorant of the fact that men born poor become wealthy, and that men born to wealth become poor; but this fact does not necessarily diminish the numbers of the poor, nor augment the numbers of the rich. The relative numbers of the two classes remain, or may remain, the same. But be this as it may; one fact is certain, no man born

poor has ever, by his wages, as a simple operative, risen to the class of the wealthy. Rich he may have become, but it has not been by his own manual labor. He has in some way contrived to tax for his benefit the labor of others. He may have accumulated a few dollars which he has placed at usury, or invested in trade; or he may, as a master workman, obtain a premium on his journeymen; or he may have from a clerk passed to a partner, or from a workman to an overseer. The simple market wages for ordinary labor, has never been adequate to raise him from poverty to wealth. This fact is decisive of the whole controversy, and proves that the system of wages must be supplanted by some other system, or else one half of the human race must forever be the virtual slaves of the other.

Now the great work for this age and the coming, is to raise up the laborer, and to realize in our own social arrangements and in the actual condition of all men, that equality between man and man, which God has established between the rights of one and those of another. In other words, our business is to emancipate the proletaries, as the past has emancipated the slaves. This is our work. There must be no class of our fellow men doomed to toil through life as mere workmen at wages. If wages are tolerated it must be, in the case of the individual operative, only under such conditions that by the time he is of a proper age to settle in life, he shall have accumulated enough to be an independent laborer on his own capital—on his own farm or in his own shop. Here is our work. How is it to be done? . . .

Now the evils of which we have complained are of a social nature. That is, they have their root in the constitution of society as it is, and they have attained to their present growth by means of social influences, the action of government, of laws, and of systems and institutions upheld by society, and of which individuals are the slaves. This being the case, it is evident that they are to be removed only by the action of society, that is, by government, for the action of society is government.

But what shall government do? Its first doing must be an *un*doing. There has been thus far quite too much government, as well as government of the wrong kind. The first act of government we want, is a still further limitation of itself. It must begin by circumscribing within narrower limits its powers. And then it must proceed to repeal all laws which bear against the laboring classes, and then to enact such laws as are necessary to enable them to maintain their equality. We have no faith in those systems of elevating the working classes, which propose to elevate them without calling in the aid of the government. We must have government, and legislation expressly directed to this end.

But again what legislation do we want so far as this country is concerned? We want first the legislation which shall free the government, whether State or Federal, from the control of the Banks. The Banks represent the interest of the employer, and therefore of necessity interests adverse to those of the employed; that is, they represent the interests of the business community in opposition to the laboring community. So long as the government remains under the control of the Banks, so long it must be in the hands of the natural enemies of the laboring classes, and may be made, nay, will be made, an instrument of depressing them yet lower. It is obvious then that, if our object be the elevation of the laboring classes, we must destroy the power of the Banks over the government, and place the government in the hands of the laboring classes themselves, or in the hands of those, if such there be, who have an identity of interest with them. But this cannot be done so long as the Banks exist. Such is the subtle influence of credit, and such the power of capital, that a banking system like ours, if sustained, necessarily and inevitably becomes the real and efficient government of the country. We have been struggling for ten years in this country against the power of the banks, struggling to free merely the Federal government from their grasp, but with humiliating success. At this moment, the contest is almost doubtful, not indeed in our mind, but in the minds of a no small portion of our countrymen. The partizans of the Banks count on certain victory. The Banks discount freely to build "log cabins," to purchase "hard cider," and to defray the expense of manufacturing enthusiasm for a cause which is at war with the interests of the people. That they will succeed, we do not for one moment believe; but that they could maintain the struggle so long, and be as strong as they now are, at the end of ten years' constant hostility, proves but all too well the power of the Banks, and their fatal influence on the political action of the community. The present character, standing, and resources of the Bank party, prove to a demonstration that the Banks must be destroyed, or the laborer not elevated. Uncompromising hostility to the whole banking system should therefore be the motto of every working man, and of every friend of Humanity. The system must be destroyed. On this point there must be no misgiving, no subterfuge, no palliation. The system is at war with the rights and interest of labor, and it must go. Every friend of the system must be marked as an enemy to his race, to his country, and especially to the laborer. No matter who he is, in what party he is found, or what name he bears, he is, in our judgment, no true democrat, as he can be no true Christian.

Following the destruction of the Banks, must come that of all monopolies, of all PRIVILEGE. There are many of these. We cannot specify them all; we therefore select only one, the greatest of them all, the privilege which some have of being born rich while others are born poor. It will be seen at once that we allude to the hereditary descent of property, an anomaly in our American system, which must be removed, or the system itself will be destroyed. We cannot now go into a discussion of this subject, but we promise to resume it at our earliest opportunity. We only say now, that as we have abolished hereditary monarchy and hereditary nobility, we must complete the work by abolishing hereditary property. A man shall have all he honestly acquires, so long as he himself belongs to the world in which he acquires it. But his power over his property must cease with his life, and his property must then become the property of the state, to be disposed of by some equitable law for the use of the generation which takes his place. Here is the principle without any of its details, and this is the grand legislative measure to which we look forward. We see no means of elevating the laboring classes which can be effectual without this. And is this a measure to be easily carried? Not at all. It will cost infinitely more than it cost to abolish either hereditary monarchy or hereditary nobility. It is a great measure, and a startling one. The rich, the business commu-

nity, will never voluntarily consent to it, and we think we know too much of human nature to believe that it will ever be effected peaceably. It will be effected only by the strong arm of physical force. It will come, if it ever come at all, only at the conclusion of war, the like of which the world as yet has never witnessed, and from which, however inevitable it may seem to the eye of philosophy, the heart of Humanity recoils with horror.

We are not ready for this measure yet. There is much previous work to be done, and we should be the last to bring it before the legislature. The time, however, has come for its free and full discussion. It must be canvassed in the public mind, and society prepared for acting on it. No doubt they who broach it, and especially they who support it, will experience a due share of contumely and abuse. They will be regarded by the part of the community they oppose, or may be thought to oppose, as "graceless varlets," against whom every man of substance should set his face. But this is not, after all, a thing to disturb a wise man, nor to deter a true man from telling his whole thought. He who is worthy of the name of man, speaks what he honestly believes the interests of his race demand, and seldom disquiets himself about what may be the consequences to himself. Men have, for what they believed the cause of God or man, endured the dungeon, the scaffold, the stake, the cross, and they can do it again, if need be. This subject must be freely, boldly, and fully discussed, whatever may be the fate of those who discuss it.

B. THE WHIGS

Henry Clay: WHIG PRINCIPLES

Henry Clay was a political leader with great popular gifts. A splendid orator, he possessed a remarkable ability to stir a crowd with visions of material growth and national greatness. Yet the fascination of his personality and the fire of his rhetoric could not prevail against Andrew Jackson. After his crushing defeat in the election of 1832, Clay continued his fight against Jackson's policies and became one of the chief architects of the Whig party formed in 1834. The selection below is from a speech that Henry Clay made in 1840 when the Whigs turned the tables on their Democratic opponents with the landside victory of the "log cabin and hard cider" campaign. We can assume that the principles which are presented in this speech represent much of the basic Whig consensus as it had been formed in the political battles of the 1830's.

WHAT are the positions of the two great parties of the present day! Modern democracy has reduced the federal theory of a strong and energetic executive to practical operation. It has turned from the people, the natural ally of genuine democracy, to the executive, and, instead of vigilance, jealousy, and distrust, has given to that department all its confidence, and made to it a virtual surrender of all the powers of government. The recognized maxim of royal infallibility is transplanted from the British monarchy into modern American democracy, and the president can do no wrong! This new school adopts, modifies, changes, renounces, renews opinions at the pleasure of the executive. Is the bank of the United States a useful and valuable institution? Yes, unanimously pronounces the democratic Legislature of Pennsylvania. The president vetoes it as a pernicious and dangerous establishment. The democratic majority in the same Legislature pronounces it to be pernicious and dangerous. The democratic majority of the House of Representatives of the United States, declares the deposits of the public money in the bank of the United States to be safe. The president says they are unsafe, and removes them. The democracy says they are unsafe, and approves the removal. The president says that a scheme of a sub-treasury is revolutionary and disorganizing. The democracy says it is revolutionary and disorganizing. The president says it is wise and salutary. The democracy says it is wise and salutary.

The whigs of 1840 stand where the republicans of 1798 stood, and where the whigs of the Revolution were, battling for liberty, for the people, for free institutions, against power, against corruption, against executive encroachments, against monarchy.

We are reproached with struggling for offices and their emoluments. If we acted on the avowed and acknowledged principle of our opponents, "that the spoils belong to the victors," we should indeed be unworthy of the support of the people. No! fellow-citizens; higher, nobler, more patriotic motives actuate the whig party. Their object is the restoration of the Constitution, the preservation of liberty, and rescue of the country. If they were governed by the sordid and selfish motives acted upon by their opponents, and unjustly imputed to them, to acquire office and emolument, they have only to change their names, and enter the presidential palace. The gate is always wide open, and the path is no narrow one which leads through it. The last comer, too, often fares best.

On a re-survey of the few past years we behold enough to sicken and sadden the hearts of true patriots. Executive encroachment has quickly followed upon executive encroachment; persons honored by public confidence, and from whom nothing but grateful and parental measures should have flowed, have inflicted stunning blow after blow, in such rapid succession, that, before the people could recover from the reeling effects of one, another has fallen heavily upon them. Had either of various instances of executive misrule stood out separate and alone, so that its enormity might have been seen and dwelt upon with composure, the condemnation of the executive would have long since been pronounced; but it has hitherto found safety and impunity in the bewildering effects of the multitude of its misdeeds. The nation has been in the condition of a man who, having gone to bed after his barn has been consumed by fire, is aroused in the morning to witness his dwelling-house wrapped in flames. So bold and presumptuous had the executive become, that, penetrating in its influence the hall

of a co-ordinate branch of the government, by means of a submissive or instructed majority of the Senate, it has caused a record of the country to be effaced and expunged, the inviolability of which was guarantied by a solemn injunction of the Constitution! And that memorable and scandalous scene was enacted only because the offensive record contained an expression of disapprobation of an executive proceeding.

If this state of things were to remain—if the progress of executive usurpation were to continue unchecked, hopeless despair would seize the public mind, or the people would be goaded to acts of open and violent resistance. But, thank God, the power of the president, fearful and rapid as its strides have been, is not yet too great for the power of the elective franchise; and a bright and glorious prospect, in the election of William Henry Harrison, has opened upon the country. The necessity of a change of rulers has deeply penetrated the hearts of the people; and we everywhere behold cheering manifestations of that happy event. The fact of his election alone, without reference to the measures of his administration, will powerfully contribute to the security and happiness of the people. It will bring assurance of the cessation of that long series of disastrous experiments which have so greatly afflicted the people. Confidence will immediately revive, credit be restored, active business will return, prices of products will rise; and the people will feel and know that, instead of their servants being occupied in devising measures for their ruin and destruction, they will be assiduously employed in promoting their welfare and prosperity.

But grave and serious measures will, unquestionably, early and anxiously command the earnest attention of the new administration. I have no authority to announce, and do not pretend to announce, the purposes of the new president. I have no knowledge of them, other than that which is accessible to every citizen. In what I shall say as to the course of a new administration, therefore, I mean to express my own sentiments, to speak for myself, without compromising any other person. Upon such an interesting occasion as this is, in the midst of the companions of my youth, or their descendants, I have felt that it is due to them and to myself, explicitly to declare my sentiments, without reserve, and to show that I have been, and, as I sincerely believe, the friends with whom I have acted have been, animated by the disinterested desire to advance the best interests of the country, and to preserve its free institutions.

The first, and, in my opinion, the most important object, which should engage the serious attention of a new administration, is that of circumscribing the executive power, and throwing around it such limitations and safeguards as will render it no longer dangerous to the public liberties.

Whatever is the work of man necessarily partakes of his imperfection, and it was not to be expected, that, with all the acknowledged wisdom and virtues of the framers of our Constitution, they could have sent forth a plan of government, so free from all defect, and so full of guaranties, that it should not, in the conflict of embittered parties and of excited passions, be perverted and misinterpreted. Misconceptions or erroneous constructions of the powers granted in the Constitution, would probably have occurred, after the lapse of many years, in seasons of entire calm, and with a regular and temperate administration of the government; but, during the last twelve years, the machine, driven by a reckless charioteer, with frightful impetuosity, has been greatly jarred and jolted, and it needs careful examination and a thorough repair.

With the view, therefore, to the fundamental character of the government itself, and especially of the executive branch, it seems to me that, either by amendments of the Constitution, when they are necessary, or by remedial legislation, when the object falls within the scope of the powers of Congress, there should be,

First, a provision to render a person ineligible to the office of President of the United States, after a service of one term.

Much observation and deliberate reflection have satisfied me that too much of the time, the thoughts, and the exertions of the incumbent, are occupied, during his first term, in securing his reelection. The public business, consequently, suffers; and measures are proposed or executed with less regard to the general prosperity than to their influence upon the approaching election. If the limitation to one term existed, the president would be exclusively devoted to the discharge of his public duties; and he would endeavor to signalize his administration by the beneficence and wisdom of its measures.

Secondly, the veto power should be more precisely defined, and be subjected to further limitations and qualifications. Although a large, perhaps the largest, proportion of all the acts of Congress, passed at the short session of Congress since the commencement of the government, were passed within the three last days of the session, and when, of course, the president for the time being had not the ten days for consideration, allowed by the Constitution, President Jackson, availing himself of that allowance, has failed to return important bills. When not returned by the president, within the ten days, it is questionable whether they are laws or not. It is very certain that the next Congress cannot act upon them by deciding whether or not they shall become laws, the president's objections notwithstanding. All this ought to be provided for.

At present, a bill, returned by the president, can only become a law by the concurrence of two thirds of the members of each House. I think if Congress passes a bill after discussion and consideration, and, after weighing the objections of the president, still believes it ought to pass, it should become a law provided a majority of *all* the members of each House concur in its passage. If the weight of his argument, and the weight of his influence conjointly, cannot prevail on a majority, against their previous convictions, in my opinion, the bill ought not to be arrested. Such is the provision of the Constitutions of several of the States, and that of Kentucky among them.

Thirdly, the power of dismission from office, should be restricted, and the exercise of it be rendered responsible.

The constitutional concurrence of the Senate is necessary to the confirmation of all important appointments; but, without consulting the Senate, without any other motive than resentment or caprice, the president may dismiss, at his sole pleasure, an officer created by the joint action of himself and the Senate. The practical effect is, to nullify the agency of the Senate. There may be, occasionally, cases in which the public interest requires an immediate dismission without waiting for the assembling of the Senate; but, in all such cases, the president should be bound to communicate fully the grounds and motives of the dismission. The power would be thus rendered responsible. Without it, the exercise of the power is utterly repugnant to free institutions, the basis of which is perfect responsibility, and dangerous to the public liberty, as has been already shown.

Fourthly, the control over the treasury of the United States should be confided and confined exclusively to Congress; and all authority of the president over it, by means of dismissing the Secretary of the Treasury, or other persons having the immediate charge of it, be rigorously precluded.

You have heard much, fellow-citizens, of the divorce of banks and government. After crippling them and impairing their utility, the executive and its partisans have systematically denounced them. The executive and the country were warned again and again of the fatal course that has been pursued; but the executive nevertheless persevered, commencing by praising, and ending by decrying, the State banks. Under cover of the smoke which has been raised, the real object all along has been, and yet is, to obtain the possession of the money power of the Union. That accomplished and sanctioned by the people—the union of the sword and the purse in the hands of the president effectually secured—and farewell to American liberty. The subtreasury is the scheme for effecting that union; and, I am told, that of all the days in the year, that which gave birth to our national existence and freedom, is the selected day to be disgraced by ushering into existence a measure imminently perilous to the liberty, which, on that anniversary, we commemorate in joyous festivals. Thus, in the spirit of destruction which animates our rulers, would they convert a day of gladness and of glory, into a day of sadness and mourning. Fellow-citizens, there is one divorce urgently demanded by the safety and the highest interests of the country—a divorce of the president from the treasury of the United States.

And, fifthly, the appointment of members of Congress to any office, or any but a few specific offices, during their continuance in office, and for one year thereafter, should be prohibited.

This is a hackneyed theme, but it is not less deserving of serious consideration. The Constitution now interdicts the appointment of a member of Congress to any office created, or the emoluments of which have been increased while he was in office. In the purer days of the republic, that restriction might have been sufficient, but in these more degenerate times, it is necessary, by an amendment of the Constitution, to give the principle greater extent.

These are the subjects, in relation to the permanent character of the government itself, which, it seems to me, are worthy of the serious attention of the people, and of a new administration. There are others of an administrative nature, which require prompt and careful consideration.

First, the currency of the country, its stability and uniform value, and as intimately and indissolubly connected with it, the insurance of the faithful performance of the fiscal services, necessary to the government, should be maintained and secured by exercising all the powers requisite to those objects with which Congress is constitutionally invested. These are the great ends to be aimed at; the means are of subordinate importance. Whether these ends, indispensable to the well-being of both the people and the government, are to be attained by sound and safe State banks, carefully selected, and properly distributed, or by a new bank of the United States, with such limitations, conditions, and restrictions, as

have been indicated by experience, should be left to the arbitrament of enlightened public opinion.

Candor and truth require me to say, that, in my judgment, while banks continue to exist in the country, the services of a bank of the United States cannot be safely dispensed with. I think that the power to establish such a bank is a settled question; settled by Washington and by Madison, by the people, by forty years' acquiescence, by the judiciary, and by both of the great parties which so long held sway in this country. I know and I respect the contrary opinion, which is entertained in this State. But, in my deliberate view of the matter, the power to establish such a bank being settled, and being a necessary and proper power, the only question is, as to the expediency of its exercise. And on questions of mere expediency, public opinion ought to have a controlling influence. Without banks, I believe we cannot have a sufficient currency; without a bank of the United States, I fear we cannot have a sound currency. But it is the end, that of a sound and sufficient currency, and a faithful execution of the fiscal duties of government, that should engage the dispassionate and candid consideration of the whole community. There is nothing in the name of the bank of the United States which has any magical charm, or to which any one need be wedded. It is to secure certain great objects, without which society cannot prosper; and if, contrary to my apprehension, these objects can be accomplished by dispensing with the agency of a bank of the United States, and employing that of State banks, all ought to rejoice, and heartily acquiesce, and none would more than I should.

Second, that the public lands, in conformity with the trusts created expressly, or by just implication, on their acquisition, be administered in a spirit of liberality toward the new States and Territories, and a spirit of justice toward all the States.

The land bill which was rejected by President Jackson, and acts of occasional legislation, will accomplish both these objects. I regret that the time does not admit of my exposing here the nefarious plans and purposes of the administration as to this vast national resource. That, like every other great interest of the country, is administered with the sole view of the effect upon the interests of the party in power. A bill has passed the Senate, and is now pending before the House, according to which, forty millions of dollars are stricken from the real value of a certain portion of the public lands by a short process; and a citizen of Virginia, residing on the south-west side of the Ohio, is not allowed to purchase lands as cheap, by half a dollar per acre, as a citizen living on the north-west side of that river. I have no hesitation in expressing my conviction, that the whole public domain is gone if Mr. Van Buren be re-elected.

Third, that the policy of protecting and encouraging the production of American industry, entering into competition with the rival productions of foreign industry, be adhered to and maintained on the basis of the principles and in the spirit of the compromise of March, 1833.

Protection and national independence are, in my opinion, identical and synonymous. The principle of abandonment of the one cannot be surrendered without a forfeiture of the other. Who, with just pride and national sensibility, can think of subjecting the products of our industry to all the taxation and restraints of foreign powers, without effort, on our part, to counteract their prohibitions and burdens, by suitable countervailing legislation? The question cannot be, ought not to be, one of principle, but of measure and degree. I adopt that of the compromise act, not because that act is irrepealable, but because it met with the sanction of the nation. Stability, with moderate and certain protection, is far more important than instability, the necessary consequence of high protection. But the protection of the compromise act will be adequate, in most, if not as to all interests. The twenty per centum which it stipulates, cash duties, home valuations, and the list of free articles inserted in the act for the particular advantage of the manufacturer, will insure, I trust, sufficient protection. All together, they will amount probably to no less than thirty per centum, a greater extent of protection than was secured prior to the act of 1828, which no one stands up to defend. Now the valuation of foreign goods is made not by the American authority, except in suspected cases, but by foreigners and abroad. They assess the value, and we the duty; but, as the duty depends, in most cases, upon the value, it is manifest that those who assess the value fix the duty. The home valuation will give our government what it rightfully possesses, both the power to ascertain the true value of the thing which it taxes, as well as the amount of that tax.

Fourth, that a strict and wise economy in the disbursement of the public money be steadily enforced; and that, to that end, all useless establishments, all unnecessary offices and places, foreign and domestic, and all extravagance, either in the collection or expenditure of the public revenue, be abolished and repressed.

I have not time to dwell on details in the application of this principle. I will say that a pruning-knife, long, broad, and sharp, should be applied to every department of the government. There is abundant scope for honest and skillful surgery. The annual expenditure may, in reasonable time, be brought down from its present amount of about forty millions to nearly one third of that sum.

Fifth, the several States have made such great and gratifying progress in their respective systems of internal improvement, and have been so aided by the distribution under the deposit act, that, in future, the erection of new roads and canals should be left to them, with such further aid only from the general government, as they would derive from the payment of the last installment under that act, from an absolute relinquishment of the right of Congress to call upon them to refund the previous installments, and from their equal and just quotas, to be received by a future distribution of the net proceeds from the sales of the public lands.

And sixth, that the right to slave property, being guarantied by the Constitution, and recognized as one of the compromises incorporated in that instrument by our ancestors, should be left where the Constitution has placed it, undisturbed and unagitated by Congress.

These, fellow-citizens, are views both of the structure of the government and of its administration, which appear to me worthy of commanding the grave attention of the public and its new servants. Although, I repeat, I have neither authority nor purpose to commit anybody else, I believe most, if not all, of them are entertained by the political friends with whom I have acted. Whether the salutary reforms which they include will be effected or considered, depends upon the issue of that great struggle which is now going on throughout all this country. This contest has had no parallel since the period of the Revolution. In both instances, there is a similarity of object. That was to achieve, this is to preserve the liberties of the country. Let us catch the spirit which animated, and imitate the virtues which adorned our noble ancestors. Their devotion, their constancy, their untiring activity, their perseverance, their indomitable resolution, their sacrifices, their valor! If they fought for liberty or death, in the memorable language of one of the most illustrious of them, let us never forget that the prize now at hazard, is liberty or slavery. We should be encouraged by the fact, that the contest, to the success of which they solemnly pledged their fortunes, their lives, and their sacred honors, was far more unequal than that in which we are engaged. But, on the other hand, let us cautiously guard against too much confidence. History and experience prove that more has been lost by self-confidence and contempt of enemies than won by skill and courage. Our opponents are powerful in numbers, and in organization, active, insidious, possessed of ample means, and wholly unscrupulous in the use of them. They count upon success by the use of two words, democracy and federalism; democracy, which, in violation of all truth, they appropriate to themselves, and federalism, which, in violation of all justice, they apply to us. And allow me to conjure you not to suffer yourselves to be diverted, deceived, or discouraged by the false rumors which will be industriously circulated, between the present time and the period of the election, by our opponents. They will put them forth in every variety, and without number, in the most imposing forms, certified and sworn to by conspicuous names. They will brag, they will boast, they will threaten. Regardless of all their arts, let us keep steadily and faithfully and fearlessly at work. . . .

Calvin Colton: LABOR AND CAPITAL

Calvin Colton is one of the more interesting intellectuals associated with American Whiggery in the Jacksonian era. After a successful career in the ministry, Colton became an editor and pamphleteer for the Whig Party. In 1842–43, he was editor of The True Whig *in Washington, and, in 1844, he became the official biographer of Henry Clay. In 1843–44, Colton wrote a series of political tracts under the name of "Junius." The ten Junius Tracts represent the most complete codification of all of the Whig positions, old and new. The following selection is taken from Junius Tract No. VII and is a remarkable example of the effort of Whig ideologists like Colton to develop a fusion of the principles of democracy and capitalism.*

1. WHAT IS LABOR?

IT is any man's or woman's efforts to live and prosper, whether of body or of mind, or of both; whether in agriculture, or commerce, or manufactures, or mechanics, or in either of the numerous branches of these great and comprehensive pursuits; whether in the useful or fine arts, in digging ditches or digging out the sciences; whether in a professional career, or in making books; in teaching, or in study; in legislation, or in government; in making pins, or casting cannon; in the use of hands or of feet, of fingers or of toes, of muscles or of brains; in search of knowledge, or in its application; in inventions, or their uses; in making canals, or building ships; erecting railroads, or constructing locomotives; in burning lime or brick, in quarrying or in masonry; in wielding a sledge-hammer, or making watches; in grinding knives, or selling brickdust; in fishing for oysters, or harpooning whales; in any one of the thousand occupations, of the city or the country, on the land or on the sea; and so on, and so on, to the end of the infinite diversity of human pursuits, by which men and women toil for a livelihood, and to get on in the world. In a free country each one chooses his own vocation, and it is not easy to say, whether mind work or muscular effort is hardest.

2. WHAT IS CAPITAL?

Money is usually called capital. But it is not exclusively so, unless it is intended to comprehend everything that will fetch money; or everything that is *worth* money. In this sense labor is capital. Labor, certainly, is the foundation and cause of wealth. All the world would be poor, and come to nothing without it. Whatever any man has, which others want, and which, being wanted, will fetch money, whether it be a capacity for labor, or any species of property, it is capital. For any man, therefore, to know how rich he is, or how much capital he has, he has only to inquire *what he can do and what he has* that will fetch money.

3. THE CAPITAL OF LABOR.

He who is able to work, and who can find employment with fair pay, is rich to begin with, and may become rich in the usual sense of the term. A power to labor, where labor is in demand, is the best, most independent, and most productive of all capital. Money at interest, or in stocks, usually produces, in this country, an income averaging perhaps six per cent. Some get more, some less, and some none at all. They are liable to go backward, and lose principal itself. But labor, with economy, can hardly ever be worth less than fifty per cent. That is, a laborer can live satisfactorily, and lay up, as vested capital, half of his wages. In some kinds of employment, he can lay up three-fourths, it may be more than that. Economy and skill in the management of his earnings, may also be made productive of wealth, in addition to the profits of his labor. Some laborers, by a careful use of past earnings, soon get to realize a hundred per cent on their capital, including labor; and then they are growing rich, wealthy. Industrious labor of any kind, in a country like ours, with economy, and being applied where labor is in demand for wages, is a sure foundation of wealth. Man does not have to labor to acquire the power. It is a capital with which he is endowed by creation, an independent faculty, and more productive than any other.

4. SKILL IN LABOR, AND IN THE MANAGEMENT OF ITS AVAILS, IS CAPITAL.

Man has not only bones, sinews, muscles, and other powers of bodily labor, but he has mind to direct it, to improve in it, to make it more available, to put all its proceeds to a profitable use, and to improve even its uses. Labor turns bodily power to account, and skill multiplies the profits of labor, so that when a man gets a-going in the world, he goes fast. Riches flow in, and wealth accumulates. A man's power of labor is limited; but his skill is unlimited. Skill is often a thousand times more productive than what is commonly called labor. But, it is to be remembered, that skill itself is the fruit of the labor of mind, or is the employment of mind, as muscular effort is labor of the body. But skill is capital. It is equally applicable to agriculture, as to manufactures; to the mechanic, or the useful, or fine arts. It is applicable to trade and commerce, to every pursuit and occupation of life.

5. ENTERPRISE IS CAPITAL.

It might seem quite unnecessary to say, in view of what enterprise has accomplished in and for this country, from the beginning of our history, that enterprise is capital. With slender means, it has evoked unbounded wealth from the long repose of a continent, and erected thereupon a vast national estate. No other species of capital has contributed so largely to this stupendous result. As the collective power of national enterprise is composed of individual enterprise, we find accordingly the same character in isolated conditions, chequering the whole surface of society with great achievements effected by single persons. There was capital enough in the soul of Washington, to humble the greatest nation, and to make another, with means that would have been laughed to scorn as a subject of prophecy. In all our history, and in the various walks of life, are to be found like miracles of enterprise, originating in the profound and inexhaustible wealth, and carried forward to consummation, by the invisible power of man's moral attributes.

* * *

7. VESTED CAPITAL.

By vested capital is commonly understood money put to use for what is called interest or income. The most common forms of vested capital, are bonds, mortgages, negotiable notes, silent partnerships in business firms, stocks in banks, insurances offices, turnpike and railroads, canals, fishing companies, great commercial enterprises, steamboats and steamships, navigation companies, manufactories, state and government securities, and any undertaking that is beyond the ordinary means of individuals, and which requires the combined and aggregate capital of numerous persons having money to put to use. The capital of corporate companies or bodies, formed for these objects, is usually divided into small shares, which, being made negotiable, that anybody can buy or sell, are thence called *stocks.*

8. CORPORATIONS.

The object of corporations is to combine the surplus or spare capital of numerous individuals, for enterprises which are usually beyond the reach of single persons. Properly organized by the statute of incorporation, by a division of the capital into small shares, and securing to men of small means equal chances, they are well adapted to a democratic state of society, by bringing down the powers of government, distributing them among the people, and vesting them in the hands of all persons who can raise twenty, or fifty, or a hundred dollars, according to the price of shares. Few and large corporations, monopolizing power in their own specific spheres, are objects of popular jealousy, and justly so. But the multiplication of them, with moderate capital and powers, divided into small shares, spreads them out over the surface of society, and whatever powers they have, be it more or less, is so much resigned by the government, and vested immediately in the hands of the people, who are able and disposed to be owners

of stock. It is a wider and more democratic distribution of power. The responsibility of the managers, is to the stockholders for the use of the capital, and to the government, and through the government, to the great body of the people, for the use of their powers. That is the best, most democratic, and most beneficent system of corporations, which enables and encourages laborers and men of small means, widows and orphans, and the more dependent and helpless portions of the community, to become interested in them, by the investment and application of their funds, which they themselves could not employ to advantage. For example:—Two men, in partnership, were joint-owners of mills of great value in the state of Maine, and one of them died, leaving a widow and several children. The widow and children, of course, could not manage such a business; but by an act of incorporation from the state, the widow and the guardians of her children became corporators and managers, and the joint-interest went on as before. It will be seen, that cases are constantly occurring in society, which require the aid of such privileges. All helpless persons, who have capital enough to support them, but who are unable to manage it, naturally resort to such helps provided by the state, in parental care, and by considerations of humanity, as well as for the general welfare.

* * *

17. A FALSE NOTION.

It has been a prevalent and fatal doctrine in this country, with a certain class of statesmen, that it is always a safe policy and a duty in the government, to fight against moneyed capitalists, in whatever place or shape they lift up their heads, whether in banks, or in manufactories, or in any and all other forms and enterprises requiring associated capital. In this, it is not considered, that the employment and thriving of the people depend on the profitable investment of the moneyed capital of the country; nor that the wages and profits of labor, and the price of its products, depend on the profits accruing from the use of the moneyed capital which labor employs. Moneyed capital is regarded by this policy as a master, not as a servant and instrument; as a hostile power, not as a friendly auxiliary; as having in itself a faculty of independence, not as deriving all its value from labor; and as aiming to acquire a supremacy over society. But a little reflection, in view of what has been said, one would think, ought to show, that the condition of moneyed capital, in this country, is *passive* in the hand of labor, and not *active* to rule *over* it, and that it is not possible to change this relation of dependence in the former on the latter. Moneyed capital, in itself, is an *inert* power, and derives all its vitality from the touch of labor. For government, therefore, to open the way, by its policy, for the profitable use of money, is the same as to provide for the success and fair reward of industry and work; and that policy which destroys the profit of money, destroys the profit of labor. Let government strike at the rich, and the blow falls on the heads of the poor.

* * *

19. COMPARATIVE VIEW OF THE POSITION OF LABOR IN AMERICA AND EUROPE.

We have told in the outset what we mean by labor. It is they who work—real workers, no matter *in* what, or *with* what *end,* if it be lawful and honorable work, to supply the wants of civilized man, or the increasing wants of advancing civilization. The more wants, the more work, and so much the better for all, where each chooses his own calling, and finds employment.

But the position of labor in this country is, in a variety of important particulars, a new one in human society. 1. It is *free*—with the exception of African slave labor. This species of freedom, which is a most important attainment in the progress of society, implies a practicable *alternative* to working on wages *at the price fixed by the employer.* In Europe, for the most part, there is no such alternative, and the laborer is *compelled* to work at a price in which he has no voice, *or he must starve;* and for the reason that he has no voice in fixing his wages, they are too scanty for comfort, much more for bettering his condition, and often too scanty for subsistence. European wages are next to a state of *starvation.* At best, it is a state of slavery, *without hope.* But in this country, labor occupies *a high social and political position.* It is never *compelled* to work for wages fixed by employers, because there is always open to it the *alternative* of working *on its own hook.* American labor, therefore, does not *accept* a price imposed, but *commands* its own price. At least, it is always an *independent* party in the compact. It is made *freely,* and can be as freely dissolved, without incurring the doom of starvation or distressing want. 2. The *social* position of American labor is such, that none but workers are held in respect—and work is held in the highest respect. No power, in this country, can enforce respect for the man who has nothing to do, and who does nothing. Just in proportion as a rich man retires from society, to wrap himself up in selfishness, does he lose his influence, and the idle, lazy poor man gets little pity in his poverty. Our fathers brought with them both the necessity and spirit of work, and made it respectable. It has been transmitted as the highest recommendation, and the most honorable character. 3. The *political* position of labor here is all-powerful, and so long as it is so, it cannot but be respectable. As a nation of workers, we *demand* from Government a security for the interests and rights of labor, and one of those rights is, that *free* American labor shall not be put on the same level with the *forced* labor of other countries, or any country. It is only necessary for the people of this country to understand correctly what the true interests and rights of labor are, and they are sure to have them secured at the ballot-box. No earthly power can hinder it. What more elevated or more commanding position, can labor possibly occupy? The free American laborer is the most powerful, and may well be the proudest of men. \

* * *

35. THE CAPACITIES OF OUR COUNTRY.

Well and rightly governed, it is capable, not only of astonishing the world, but of astonishing itself. If things do not go on well, it must be owing solely to the perversion of our institutions from their design. There is no sufficient apology, that our general prosperity should *ever* be interrupted. It is impossible that it should be, except by a violation or misapplication of the trusts reposed in our public functionaries. By a suitable protection of the interests of American labor and industry, from a self-sacrificing rivalship with a foreign, oppressed, and degraded pauperism, which is in no wise mitigated, but only aggravated and rendered more hopeless by the favor done to their oppressors; by a proper encouragement of the voluntary enterprises of our own citizens, the people of this country, with the rich and inexhaustible treasures of creation comprehended in our jurisdiction, are capable of producing amazing results. That almost astonishing

height of prosperity, to which we had attained, under all the disadvantages of a defective tariff system, before the advent of the late Destructive Dynasty, is conclusive and impressive evidence of what this nation is capable of under a wise and faithful administration of our public affairs. We had been put in a train, by which we were enabled to discharge with ease the entire and heavy debt incurred by the last war with Great Britain, and to overwhelm the public treasury with surplus funds; the public domain in the west was in such demand, that the sales of one year amounted to *twenty-four millions of dollars,* and although there were special reasons for this fact, which could not be expected to operate in perpetuity, to an equal extent, nevertheless, in a prosperous state of things, there would be a steady increase in those sales, which, under an equitable system of distributing the proceeds among the States, whose property they are, would relieve the burdens of the indebted States, and give the others a chance for such enterprises as might best promote their interests.

36. THE CHANCES OF LIFE IN
THIS COUNTRY.

Ours is a country, where men start from an humble origin, and from small beginnings rise gradually in the world, as the reward of merit and industry, and where they can attain to the most elevated positions, or acquire a large amount of wealth, according to the pursuits they elect for themselves. No exclusive privileges of birth, no entailment of estates, no civil or political disqualifications, stand in their path; but one has as good a chance as another, according to his talents, prudence, and personal exertions. This is a country of *self-made men,* than which nothing better could be said of any state of society.

C. THE EUROPEANS

Alexis de Tocqueville: THE POWER OF THE MAJORITY
AND THE PURSUIT OF INDUSTRIAL CALLINGS

Alexis de Tocqueville, born in Paris and trained in the law, was sent to the United States in 1831 by the French government to investigate the prison reforms of America. But the young liberal aristocrat was interested in much more than the penal system of America. He was an intelligent observer of all the institutions, ideas, and prejudices of American democracy. Tocqueville's Democracy in America won instant recognition as a political and sociological treatise of the first rank when the two volumes appeared in 1835 and 1840. In America, the merits of the work were warmly debated by the Jacksonian generation and controversy about Tocqueville's methods and judgments has continued among historians and social scientists to the present day. Because of the abstractness of many of Tocqueville's explanations of democracy, there are difficulties in using his volumes as a historical source for the Jacksonian period. Also, even though Tocqueville was a liberal aristocrat, he was not always able to overcome his inbred aristocratic prejudices. Nevertheless, we cannot afford to neglect Tocqueville as a historical source and the following two selections give us a valuable understanding of some of the political characteristics and the social goals of Americans in the Jacksonian era.

UNLIMITED POWER OF THE MAJORITY IN THE UNITED STATES, AND ITS CONSEQUENCES

THE very essence of democratic government consists in the absolute sovereignty of the majority; for there is nothing in democratic states which is capable of resisting it. Most of the American constitutions have sought to increase this natural strength of the majority by artificial means.

The legislature is, of all political institutions, the one which is most easily swayed by the will of the majority. The Americans determined that the members of the legislature should be elected by the people *directly*, and for a *very brief term*, in order to subject them, not only to the general convictions, but even to the daily passions, of their constituents. The members of both houses are taken from the same classes in society, and nominated in the same manner; so that the movements of the legislative bodies are almost as rapid, and quite as irresistible, as those of a single assembly. It is to a legislature thus constituted, that almost all the authority of the government has been entrusted.

At the same time that the law increased the strength of those authorities which of themselves were strong, it en-

From Alexis de Tocqueville, *Democracy in America*, Francis Bowen, ed., Cambridge, Mass., 1863, Vol. I, pp. 324–327, 332, 340–343; Vol. II, pp. 187–192.

feebled more and more those which were naturally weak. It deprived the representatives of the executive power of all stability and independence; and, by subjecting them completely to the caprices of the legislature, it robbed them of the slender influence which the nature of a democratic government might have allowed them to exercise. In several States, the judicial power was also submitted to the election of the majority; and in all of them, its existence was made to depend on the pleasure of the legislative authority, since the representatives were empowered annually to regulate the stipend of the judges.

Custom has done even more than law. A proceeding is becoming more and more general in the United States, which will, in the end, do away with the guaranties of representative government: it frequently happens that the voters, in electing a delegate, point out a certain line of conduct to him, and impose upon him certain positive obligations which he is pledged to fulfill. With the exception of the tumult, this comes to the same thing as if the majority itself held its deliberations in the market-place.

Several other circumstances concur to render the power of the majority in America not only preponderant, but irresistible. The moral authority of the majority is partly based upon the notion, that there is more intelligence and wisdom in a number of men united than in a single individual, and that the number of the legislators is more important than their quality. The theory of equality is thus applied to the intellects of men; and human pride is thus assailed in its last retreat by a doctrine which the minority hesitate to admit, and to which they will but slowly assent. Like all other powers, and perhaps more than any other, the authority of the many requires the sanction of time in order to appear legitimate. At first, it enforces obedience by constraint; and its laws are not *respected* until they have been long maintained.

The right of governing society, which the majority supposes itself to derive from its superior intelligence, was introduced into the United States by the first settlers; and this idea, which of itself would be sufficient to create a free nation, has now been amalgamated with the manners of the people and the minor incidents of social life.

The French, under the old monarchy, held it for a maxim that the king could do no wrong; and if he did do wrong, the blame was imputed to his advisers. This notion made obedience very easy; it enabled the subject to complain of the law, without ceasing to love and honor the lawgiver. The Americans entertain the same opinion with respect to the majority.

The moral power of the majority is founded upon yet another principle, which is, that the interests of the many are to be preferred to those of the few. It will readily be perceived that the respect here professed for the rights of the greater number must naturally increase or diminish according to the state of parties. When a nation is divided into several great irreconcilable interests, the privilege of the majority is often overlooked, because it is intolerable to comply with its demands.

If there existed in America a class of citizens whom the legislating majority sought to deprive of exclusive privileges which they had possessed for ages, and to bring down from an elevated station to the level of the multitude, it is probable that the minority would be less ready to submit to its laws. But as the United States were colonized by men holding equal rank, there is as yet no natural or permanent disagreement between the interests of its different inhabitants.

There are communities in which the members of the minority can never hope to draw over the majority to their side, because they must then give up the very point which is at issue between them. Thus, an aristocracy can never become a majority whilst it retains its exclusive privileges, and it cannot cede its privileges without ceasing to be an aristocracy.

In the United States, political questions cannot be taken up in so general and absolute a manner; and all parties are willing to recognize the rights of the majority, because they all hope at some time to be able to exercise them to their own advantage. The majority, therefore, in that country, exercise a prodigious actual authority, and a power of opinion which is nearly as great; no obstacles exist which can impede or even retard its progress, so as to make it heed the complaints of those whom it crushes upon its path. This state of things is harmful in itself, and dangerous for the future. . . .

Unlimited power is in itself a bad and dangerous thing. Human beings are not competent to exercise it with discretion. God alone can be omnipotent, because his wisdom and his justice are always equal to his power. There is no power on earth so worthy of honor in itself, or clothed with rights so sacred, that I would admit its uncontrolled and all-predominant authority. When I see that the right and the means of absolute command are conferred on any power whatever, be it called a people or a king, an aristocracy or a democracy, a monarchy or a republic, I say there is the germ of tyranny, and I seek to live elsewhere, under other laws.

In my opinion, the main evil of the present democratic institutions of the United States does not arise, as is often asserted in Europe, from their weakness, but from their irresistible strength. I am not so much alarmed at the excessive liberty which reigns in that country, as at the inadequate securities which one finds there against tyranny.

When an individual or a party is wronged in the United States, to whom can he apply for redress? If to public opinion, public opinion constitutes the majority; if to the legislature, it represents the majority, and implicitly obeys it; if to the executive power, it is appointed by the majority, and serves as a passive tool in its hands. The public force consists of the majority under arms; the jury is the majority invested with the right of hearing judicial cases; and in certain States, even the judges are elected by the majority. However iniquitous or absurd the measure of which you complain, you must submit to it as well as you can. . . .

The tendencies which I have just mentioned are as yet but slightly perceptible in political society; but they already exercise an unfavorable influence upon the national character of the Americans. I attribute the small number of distinguished men in political life to the ever-increasing despotism of the majority in the United States.

When the American Revolution broke out, they arose in great numbers; for public opinion then served, not to tyrannize over, but to direct the exertions of individuals. Those celebrated men, sharing the agitation of mind common at that period, had a grandeur peculiar to themselves, which was reflected back upon the nation, but was by no means borrowed from it.

In absolute governments, the great nobles who are nearest to the throne flatter the passions of the sovereign, and voluntarily truckle to his caprices. But the mass of the nation does not degrade itself by servitude; it often submits from weakness, from habit, or from ignorance, and sometimes from loyalty. Some nations have been known to sacrifice their own desires to those of the sovereign with pleasure and pride, thus exhibiting a sort of independence of mind in the very act of submission. These nations are miserable, but they are not degraded. There is a great difference between doing what one does not approve, and feigning to approve what one does; the one is the weakness of a feeble person, the other befits the temper of a lackey.

In free countries, where every one is more or less called upon to give his opinion on affairs of state—in democratic republics, where public life is incessantly mingled with domestic affairs, where the sovereign authority is accessible on every side, and where its attention can always be attracted by vociferation—more persons are to be met with who speculate upon its weaknesses, and live upon ministering to its passions, than in absolute monarchies. Not because men are naturally worse in these states than elsewhere, but the temptation is stronger and of easier access at the same time. The result is a more extensive debasement of character.

Democratic republics extend the practice of currying favor with the many, and introduce it into all classes at once: this is the most serious reproach that can be addressed to them. This is especially true in democratic states organized like the American republics, where the power of the majority is so absolute and irresistible that one must give up his rights as a citizen, and almost abjure his qualities as a man, if he intends to stray from the track which it prescribes.

In that immense crowd which throngs the avenues to power in the United States, I found very few men who displayed that manly candor and masculine independence of opinion which frequently distinguished the Americans in former times, and which constitutes the leading feature in distinguished characters wheresoever they may be found. It seems, at first sight, as if all the minds of the Americans were formed upon one model, so accurately do they follow the same route. A stranger does, indeed, sometimes meet with Americans who dissent from the rigor of these formularies—with men who deplore the defects of the laws, the mutability and the ignorance of democracy—who even go so far as to observe the evil tendencies which impair the national character, and to point out such remedies as it might be possible to apply; but no one is there to hear them except yourself, and you, to whom these secret reflections are confided, are a stranger and a bird of passage. They are very ready to communicate truths which are useless to you, but they hold a different language in public.

If ever these lines are read in America, I am well assured of two things—in the first place, that all who peruse them will raise their voices to condemn me; and, in the second place, that many of them will acquit me at the bottom of their conscience.

I have heard of patriotism in the United States, and I have found true patriotism among the people, but never among the leaders of the people. This may be explained by analogy: despotism debases the oppressed much more than the oppressor: in absolute monarchies, the king often has great virtues, but the courtiers are invariably servile. It is true that American courtiers do not say "Sire," or "Your Majesty"—a distinction without a difference. They are forever talking of the natural intelligence of the people whom they serve: they do not debate the question which of the virtues of their master is pre-eminently worthy of admiration, for they assure him that he possesses all the virtues without having acquired them, or without caring to acquire them; they do not give him their daughters and their wives to be raised at his pleasure to the rank of his concubines; but, by sacrificing their opinions, they prostitute themselves. Moralists and philosophers in America are not obliged to conceal their opinions under the veil of allegory; but before they venture upon a harsh truth, they say, "We are aware that the people whom we are addressing are too superior to the weaknesses of human nature to lose the command of their temper for an instant. We should not hold this language if we were not speaking to men whom their virtues and their intelligence render more worthy of freedom than all the rest of the world." The sycophants of Louis XIV could not flatter more dexterously.

For my part, I am persuaded that, in all governments, whatever their nature may be, servility will cower to force, and adulation will follow power. The only means of preventing men from degrading themselves is to invest no one with that unlimited authority which is the sure method of debasing them. . . .

WHAT CAUSES ALMOST ALL AMERICANS TO FOLLOW INDUSTRIAL CALLINGS

Agriculture is, perhaps, of all the useful arts, that which improves most slowly amongst democratic nations. Frequently, indeed, it would seem to be stationary, because other arts are making rapid strides towards perfection. On the other hand, almost all the tastes and habits which the equality of condition produces naturally lead men to commercial and industrial occupations.

Suppose an active, enlightened, and free man, enjoying a competency, but full of desires: he is too poor to live in idleness; he is rich enough to feel himself protected from the immediate fear of want, and he thinks how he can better his condition. This man has conceived a taste for physical gratifications, which thousands of his fellow-men indulge in around him; he has himself begun to enjoy these pleasures, and he is eager to increase his means of satisfying these tastes more completely. But life is slipping away, time is urgent—to what is he to turn? The cultivation of the ground promises an almost certain result to his exertions, but a slow one; men are not enriched by it without patience and toil. Agriculture is therefore only suited to those who have already large superfluous wealth, or to those whose penury bids them only seek a bare subsistence. The choice of such a man as we have supposed is soon made; he sells his plot of ground, leaves his dwelling, and embarks in some hazardous but lucrative calling.

Democratic communities abound in men of this kind; and, in proportion as the equality of conditions becomes greater, their multitude increases. Thus, democracy not only swells the number of workingmen, but it leads men to prefer one kind of labor to another; and, whilst it diverts them from agriculture, it encourages their taste for commerce and manufactures.

This spirit may be observed even amongst the richest members of the community. In democratic countries, however opulent a man is supposed to be, he is almost always discontented with his fortune, because he finds that he is less rich than his father was, and he fears that his sons will be less rich than himself. Most rich men in democracies are therefore constantly haunted by the desire of obtaining wealth, and they naturally turn their attention to trade and manufactures, which appear to offer the readiest and most efficient means of success. In this respect, they share the instincts of the poor without feeling the same necessities; say, rather, they feel the most imperious of all necessities, that of not sinking in the world.

In aristocracies, the rich are at the same time the governing power. The attention which they unceasingly devote to important public affairs diverts them from the lesser cares which trade and manufactures demand. But if an individual happens to turn his attention to business, the will of the body to which he belongs will immediately prevent him from pursuing it; for, however men may declaim against the rule of numbers, they cannot wholly escape it; and even amongst those aristocratic bodies which most obstinately refuse to acknowledge the rights of the national majority, a private majority is formed which governs the rest.

In democratic countries, where money does not lead those who possess it to political power, but often removes them from it, the rich do not know how to spend their leisure. They are driven into active life by the inquietude and the greatness of their desires, by the extent of their resources, and by the taste for what is extraordinary, which is almost always felt by those who rise, by whatsoever means, above the crowd. Trade is the only road open to them. In democracies, nothing is more great or more brilliant than commerce: it attracts the attention of the public, and fills the imagination of the multitude; all energetic passions are directed towards it. Neither their own prejudices nor those of anybody else can prevent the rich from devoting themselves to it. The wealthy members of democracies never form a body which has manners and regulations of its own; the opinions peculiar to their class do not restrain them, and the common opinions of their country urge them on. Moreover, as all the large fortunes which are found in a democratic community are of commercial growth, many generations must succeed each other before their possessors can have entirely laid aside their habits of business.

Circumscribed within the narrow space which politics leaves them, rich men in democracies eagerly embark in commercial enterprise: there they can extend and employ their natural advantages; and indeed, it is even by the boldness and the magnitude of their industrial speculations that we may measure the slight esteem in which productive industry would have been held by them, if they had been born amidst an aristocracy.

A similar observation is likewise applicable to all men living in democracies, whether they be poor or rich. Those who live in the midst of democratic fluctuations have always before their eyes the image of chance; and they end by liking all undertakings in which chance plays a part. They are therefore all led to engage in commerce, not only for the sake of the profit it holds out to them, but for the love of the constant excitement occasioned by that pursuit.

The United States of America have only been emancipated for half a century from the state of colonial dependence in which they stood to Great Britain: the number of large fortunes there is small, and capital is still scarce. Yet no people in the world have made such rapid progress in trade and manufactures as the Americans: they constitute at the present day the second maritime nation in the world; and although their manufactures have to struggle with almost insurmountable natural impediments, they are not prevented from making great and daily advances.

In the United States, the greatest undertakings and speculations are executed without difficulty, because the whole population are engaged in productive industry, and because the poorest as well as the most opulent members of the commonwealth are ready to combine their efforts for these purposes. The consequence is, that a stranger is constantly amazed by the immense public works executed by a nation which contains, so to speak, no rich men. The Americans arrived but as yesterday on the territory which they inhabit, and they have already changed the whole order of nature for their own advantage. They have joined the Hudson to the Mississippi, and made the Atlantic Ocean communicate with the Gulf of Mexico, across a continent of more than five hundred leagues in extent which separates the two seas. The longest railroads which have been constructed, up to the present time, are in America.

But what most astonishes me in the United States is not so much the marvelous grandeur of some undertakings, as the innumerable multitude of small ones. Almost all the farmers of the United States combine some trade with agriculture; most of them make agriculture itself a trade. It seldom happens that an American farmer settles for good upon the land which he occupies; especially in the districts of the Far West, he brings land into tillage in order to sell it again, and not to farm it: he builds a farm-house on the speculation, that, as the state of the country will soon be changed by the increase of population, a good price may be obtained for it.

Every year, a swarm of people from the North arrive in the Southern States, and settle in the parts where the cotton-plant and the sugar-cane grow. These men cultivate the soil in order to make it produce in a few years enough to enrich them; and they already look forward to the time when they may return home to enjoy the competency thus acquired. Thus the Americans carry their business-like qualities into agriculture; and their trading passions are displayed in that, as in their other pursuits.

The Americans make immense progress in productive industry, because they all devote themselves to it at once; and for this same reason, they are exposed to unexpected and formidable embarrassments. As they are all engaged in commerce, their commercial affairs are affected by such various and complex causes, that it is impossible to foresee what difficulties may arise. As they are all more or less engaged in productive industry, at the least shock given to business, all private fortunes are put in jeopardy at the same time, and the state is shaken. I believe that the return of these commercial panics is an endemic disease of the democratic nations of our age. It may be rendered less dangerous, but it cannot be cured; because it does not originate in accidental circumstances, but in the temperament of these nations.

Harriet Martineau: PARTIES

*Harriet Martineau was born in a Unitarian household in Norwich,
England, and grew up in the religious intensity of an English nonconformist family. By the time she was twenty, she was determined to
leave it to other women to sew shirts and darn stockings; hence she
began to write religious essays and to prepare books of devotional ex-
ercises. Her restless mind soon turned to other subjects, and, in 1832,
she published a popularized version of the ideas of Adam Smith, Malthus, and Ricardo under the title,* Illustrations of Political Economy.
*The success of this book was sensationally swift, and Harriet Martineau
became an influential addition to a growing group of English writers
interested in reforms of various kinds. Curious to see the institutions of
a new society, she visited America in 1834–35; subsequently, she published a two volume work entitled,* Society in America. *In the selection
from this work which follows, it is readily apparent that Harriet Martineau's nonconformist and reformist temperament makes her more
sympathetic to the power of the democratic majority than Tocqueville.*

THE first gentleman who greeted me
on my arrival in the United States, a
few minutes after I had landed, informed
me without delay, that I had arrived at
an unhappy crisis, that the institutions
of the country would be in ruins before
my return to England; that the levelling
spirit was desolating society; and that the
United States were on the verge of a military despotism. This was so very like
what I had been accustomed to hear at
home, from time to time, since my childhood, that I was not quite so much
alarmed as I might have been without
such prior experience. It was amusing too
to find America so veritably the daughter
of England.

I looked around me carefully, in all
my travels, till I reached Washington,
but could see no signs of despotism; even
less of military. Except the officers and
cadets at West Point, and some militia
on a training day at Saugerties, higher up
on the Hudson, I saw nothing that could
be called military; and officers, cadets,
and militia appeared all perfectly inno-
cent of any design to seize upon the government. At Washington, I ventured to
ask an explanation from one of the most
honoured statesmen now living; who
told me, with a smile, that the country
had been in "a crisis" for fifty years past;
and would be for fifty years to come.

This information was my comfort,
from day to day, till I became sufficiently
acquainted with the country to need such
support no longer. Mournful predictions,
like that I have quoted, were made so
often, that it was easy to learn how they
originated.

In the United States, as elsewhere,
there are, and have always been, two
parties in politics, whom it is difficult to
distinguish on paper, by a statement of
their principles, but whose course of action may, in any given case, be pretty

From Harriet Martineau, *Society in America,* New York, 1837, Vol. I, pp. 8–15, 22–23.

confidently anticipated. It is remarkable how nearly their positive statements of political doctrine agree, while they differ in almost every possible application of their common principles. Close and continued observation of their agreements and differences is necessary before the British traveller can fully comprehend their mutual relation. In England, the differences of parties are so broad—between those who would have the people governed for the convenience of their rulers; those who would have the many governed, for their good, by the will of the few; and those who would have the people govern themselves—that it is, for some time, difficult to comprehend how there should be party differences as wide in a country where the first principle of government is that the people are to govern themselves. The case, however, becomes clear in time; and, amidst a half century of "crises," the same order and sequence become discernible which run through the whole course of human affairs.

As long as men continue as differently organized as they now are, there will be two parties under every government. Even if their outward fortunes could be absolutely equalized there would be, from individual constitution alone, an aristocracy and a democracy in every land. The fearful by nature would compose an aristocracy, the hopeful by nature a democracy, were all other causes of divergence done away. When to these constitutional differences are added all those outward circumstances which go to increase the fear and the hope, the mutual misunderstandings of parties are no longer to be wondered at. Men who have gained wealth, whose hope is fulfilled, and who fear loss by change, are naturally of the aristocratic class. So are men of learning, who, unconsciously identifying learning and wisdom, fear the elevation of the ignorant to a station like their own. So are men of talent, who, having gained the power which is the fit recompense of achievement, dread the having to yield it to numbers instead of desert. So are many more who feel the almost universal fear of having to part with educational prejudices, with doctrines with which honoured teachers nourished the pride of youth, and prepossessions inwoven with all that has been to them most pure, lofty, and graceful. Out of these a large aristocratic class must everywhere be formed.

Out of the hopeful—the rising, not the risen—the aspiring, not the satisfied—must a still larger class be everywhere formed. It will include all who have most to gain and least to lose; and most of those who, in the present state of education, have gained their knowledge from actual life, rather than, or as well as, from books. It will include the adventurers of society, and also the philanthropists. It will include, moreover—an accession small in number, but inestimable in power—the men of genius. It is characteristic of genius to be hopeful and aspiring. It is characteristic of genius to break up the artificial arrangements of conventionalism, and to view mankind in true perspective, in their gradations of inherent rather than of adventitious worth. Genius is therefore essentially democratic, and has always been so, whatever titles its gifted ones may have worn, or on whatever subjects they may have exercised their gifts. To whatever extent men of genius have been aristocratic, they have been so in spite of their genius, not in consistency with it. The instances are so few, and their deviations from the democratic principle so small, that men of genius must be considered as included in the democratic class.

Genius being rare, and its claims but

tardily allowed by those who have attained greatness by other means, it seems as if the weight of influence possessed by the aristocratic party—by that party which, generally speaking, includes the wealth, learning, and talents of the country—must overpower all opposition. If this is found not to be the case, if it be found that the democratic party has achieved everything that has been achieved since the United States' constitution began to work, it is no wonder that there is panic in many hearts, and that I heard from so many tongues of the desolations of the "levelling spirit," and the approaching ruin of political institutions.

These classes may be distinguished in another way. The description which Jefferson gave of the federal and republican parties of 1799 applies to the federal and democratic parties of this day, and to the aristocratic and democratic parties of every time and country. "One," says Jefferson, "fears most the ignorance of the people; the other, the selfishness of rulers independent of them."

There is much reason in both these fears. The unreasonableness of party lies in entertaining the one fear, and not the other. No argument is needed to prove that rulers are prone to selfishness and narrowness of views: and no one can have witnessed the injuries that the poor suffer in old countries—the education of hardship and insult that furnishes them with their only knowledge of the highest classes, without being convinced, that their ignorance is to be feared—their ignorance, not so much of books as of liberty and law. In old countries, the question remains open whether the many should, on account of their ignorance, be kept still in a state of political servitude, as some declare; or whether they should be gradually prepared for political freedom, as others think, by an amelioration of their condition, and by being educated in schools; or whether, as yet others maintain, the exercise of political rights and duties be not the only possible political education. In the New World, no such question remains to be debated. It has no large, degraded, injured, dangerous (white) class who can afford the slightest pretence for a panic-cry about agrarianism. Throughout the prodigious expanse of that country, I saw no poor *men,* except a few intemperate ones. I saw some very poor *women;* but God and man know that the time has not come for women to make their injuries even heard of. I saw no beggars but two professional ones, who are making their fortunes in the streets of Washington. I saw no table spread, in the lowest order of houses, that had not meat and bread on it. Every factory child carries its umbrella; and pig-drivers wear spectacles. With the exception of the foreign paupers on the seaboard, and those who are steeped in sensual vice, neither of which classes can be politically dangerous, there are none who have not the same interest in the security of property as the richest merchant of Salem, or planter of Louisiana. Whether the less wealthy class will not be the first to draw out from reason and experience the true philosophy of property, is another question. All we have to do with now is their equal interest with their richer neighbours in the security of property, in the present state of society. Law and order are as important to the man who holds land for the subsistence of his family, or who earns wages that he may have land of his own to die upon, as to any member of the president's cabinet.

Nor is there much more to fear from the ignorance of the bulk of the people in the United States, than from their poverty. It is too true that there is much ignorance; so much as to be an ever-present peril. Though, as a whole, the nation is, probably, better informed than any other entire nation, it cannot be denied that their knowledge is far inferior to what their safety and their virtue require. But *whose* ignorance is it? And ignorance of *what?* If the professors of colleges have book-knowledge, which the owner of a log-house has not; the owner of a log-house has very often, as I can testify, a knowledge of natural law, political rights, and economical fact, which the college-professor has not. I often longed to confront some of each class, to see whether there was any common ground on which they could meet. If not, the one might bring the charge of ignorance as justly as the other. If a common ground could be discovered, it would have been in their equal relation to the government under which they live; in which case, the natural conclusion would be, that each understood his own interests best, and neither could assume superiority over the other. The particular ignorance of the countryman may expose him to be flattered and cheated by an oratorical office-seeker, or a dishonest newspaper. But, on the other hand, the professor's want of knowledge of the actual affairs of the many, and his educational biases, are just as likely to cause him to vote contrary to the public interest. No one who has observed society in America will question the existence or the evil of ignorance there: but neither will he question that such real knowledge as they have is pretty fairly shared among them.

I travelled by wagon, with a party of friends, in the interior of Ohio. Our driver must be a man of great and various knowledge, if he questions all strangers as he did us, and obtains as copious answers. He told us where and how he lived, of his nine children, of his literary daughters, and the pains he was at to get books for them; and of his hopes from his girl of fourteen, who writes poetry, which he keeps a secret, lest she should be spoiled. He told us that he seldom lets his fingers touch a novel, because the consequence always is that his business stands still till the novel is finished; "and that doesn't suit." He recited to us, Pope's "Happy the man whose wish and care," &c. saying that it suited his idea exactly. He asked both the ladies present whether they had written a book. Both had; and he carried away the titles, that he might buy the books for his daughters. This man is fully informed of the value of the Union, as we had reason to perceive; and it is difficult to see why he is not as fit as any other man to choose the representatives of his interests. . . .

As an antagonist case, take the wailings of a gentleman of very distinguished station in a highly aristocratic section of society—wailings over the extent of the suffrage.

"What an enormity it is that such a man as Judge——, there, should stand on no higher level in politics than the man that grooms his horse!"

"Why should he? I suppose they have both got all they want—full representation: and they thus bear precisely the same relation to the government."

"No; the judge seldom votes, because of his office: while his groom can, perhaps, carry nineteen men to vote as he pleases. It is monstrous!"

"It seems monstrous that the judge should omit his political duty for the sake of his office; and also that nineteen men should be led by one. But limiting the suffrage would not mend the matter. Would it not do better to teach all the parties their duty?"

Let who will, choose between the wagon-driver and the scholar. Each will vote according to his own views; and the event—the ultimate majority—will prove which is so far the wiser. . . .

One of the most painful apprehensions seems to be that the poorer will heavily tax the richer members of society; the rich being always a small class. If it be true, as all parties appear to suppose, that rulers in general are prone to use their power for selfish purposes, there remains the alternative, whether the poor shall over-tax the rich, or whether the rich shall over-tax the poor: and, if one of these evils were necessary, few would doubt which would be the least. But the danger appears much diminished on the consideration that, in the country under our notice, there are not, nor are likely to be, the wide differences in property which exist in old countries. There is no class of hereditary rich or poor. Few are very wealthy; few are poor; and every man has a fair chance of being rich. No such unequal taxation has yet been ordained by the sovereign people; nor does there appear to be any danger of it, while the total amount of taxation is so very small as in the United States, and the interest that everyone has in the protection of property is so great. A friend in the South, while eulogizing to me the state of society there, spoke with compassion of his northern fellow citizens, who were exposed to the risks of "a perpetual struggle between pauperism and property." To which a northern friend replied, that it is true that there is a perpetual struggle everywhere between pauperism and property. The question is, which succeeds? In the United States, the prospect is that each will succeed. Paupers may

obtain what they want, and proprietors will keep that which they have. As a mere matter of convenience, it is shorter and easier to obtain property by enterprise and labour in the United States, than by pulling down the wealthy. Even the most desponding do not consider the case as very urgent, at present. I asked one of my wealthy friends, who was predicting that in thirty years his children would be living under a despotism, why he did not remove. "Where," said he, with a countenance of perplexity, "could I be better off?"—which appeared to me a truly reasonable question.

In a country, the fundamental principle of whose politics is, that its "rulers derive their just powers from the consent of the governed," it is clear that there can be no narrowing of the suffrage. However earnestly some may desire this, no one hopes it. But it does not follow that the apprehensive minority has nothing left but discontent. The enlightenment of society remains not only matter for hope, but for achievement. The prudent speak of the benefits of education as a matter of policy, while the philanthropic promote it as a matter of justice. Security of person and property follows naturally upon a knowledge of rights. However the aristocracy of wealth, learning, and talent may differ among themselves, as to what is the most valuable kind of knowledge, all will agree that every kind will strengthen the bonds of society. In this direction must the aristocracy work for their own security. If they sufficiently provide the means of knowledge to the community, they may dismiss their fears, and rest assured that the great theory of their government will bear any test; and that "the majority will be in the right." . . .

Francis J. Grund: THE GENIUS OF JACKSON

Grund was another European observer who was moved to write about American society in the Jacksonian era. Born in Austria, he had studied in Vienna and then migrated to America where he carried on an active career in journalism and in the writing of elementary text-books for American schools. In 1837, he issued his first work in America, The Americans in their Moral, Social, and Political Relations, *and in 1839, the two volumes of his* Aristocracy in America *were published in England. The selection which follows is taken from* Aristocracy in America *and is an account of a conversation that Grund had with two Democratic senators about the the reasons for Jackson's political success. There is much in this selection which anticipates the modern analysis of Jackson's qualities of leadership.*

GENERAL Jackson," said one of the senators, "understands the people of the United States twenty times better than his antagonists; and, if his successor have but half the same tact, the Whigs may give up the hope of governing the country for the next half century."

"You ought not to say '*tact*,'" interrupted the other senator, "for that alone will not do it; he must have the same manners as our present President. General Jackson has a peculiar way of addressing himself to the feelings of every man with whom he comes in contact. His simple unostentatious manners carry into every heart the conviction of his honesty; while the firmness of his character inspires his friends with the hope of success. His motto always was, '*Never sacrifice a friend to an enemy*,' or, '*Make yourself strong with your friends, and you need not fear your foes*.' These things, however, must be born with a man; they must be spontaneous, and felt as such by the people, or they lose the best part of their effect. All the tact in the world will not answer the same pur-

pose; for, in exactly the same proportion as we perceive a man is prudent, we become cautious ourselves, and then farewell to popularity!

"When the people give their suffrages to a man, they never do so on a rigid examination of his political principles; for this task the labouring classes of any country neither have the time nor the disposition, and it is wholly needless to attempt to persuade them to a different course by a long and tedious argument. The large masses act in politics pretty much as they do in religion. Every doctrine is with them, more or less, a matter of *faith;* received, principally, on account of their trust in the apostle. If the latter fail to captivate their hearts, no reasoning in the world is capable of filling the vacancy: and the more natural and uncorrupt the people are, the less are they to be moved by abstract reasoning, whether the form of government be republican, monarchical, or despotic."

"Precisely so," ejaculated the member. "General Jackson is popular, just because he is General Jackson; so much so, that if a man were to say a word against him in the Western States, he would be *'knocked into eternal smash.'* "

"And this sort of popularity," continued the senator, "our Northern people consider as the mere consequence of the battle of New Orleans. The battle, and General Jackson's military character, had undoubtedly a great deal to do with it; but they were not of themselves sufficient to elevate him to the Presidency. In a country in which so large a portion of the people consider the acquiring of a fortune the only rational object of pursuit—in which so great and so exclusive an importance is attached to money, that, with a few solitary exceptions, it is the only means of arriving at personal distinction—a character like Jackson's, so perfectly disinterested, and so entirely devoted to what he at least deemed the good of his country, could not but excite astonishment and admiration among the natural, and therefore more susceptible, people of the Western States. The appearance of General Jackson was a phenomenon, and would at the present time have been one in every country. He called himself 'the people's friend,' and gave proofs of his sincerity and firmness in *adhering* to his friends, and of his power to protect them. The people believed in General Jackson as much as the Turks in their prophet, and would have followed him wherever he chose to lead them. With this species of popularity it is in vain to contend; and it betrays little knowledge of the world, and the springs of human action, to believe those who possess it men of ordinary capacity.

"What the French call *'le génie du caractère,'* which is the true talisman of popular favour, is perhaps the highest talent with which mortals can be endowed. It is a pure gift of Heaven, and has accomplished the noblest deeds in history. When Napoleon reproached Voltaire with not having sufficiently appreciated the character of Mahomed, whom the French poet introduced in the drama of the same name as a mere impostor, he felt that none but a great mind could have conceived and executed what to ordinary men would have appeared absurd or chimerical; and that he who had the power to instil a lasting enthusiasm for a new cause into millions, and on that enthusiasm to establish an empire which has spread over half the world, must have been more than a mere charlatan, for he must have been possessed of a thorough knowledge of human character. This is a thing a man cannot acquire by study, if he do not possess it by intuition; and hence it can neither be defined nor understood by men not similarly gifted, who, applying their own scale to what is truly incommensurable, are always astonished at the success of those whom they were all their lives accustomed to look upon as second- or third-rate men.

"Have we not heard it objected to Napoleon, that he could not write an elegant epistle? Do the French not pity Shakespeare for having been so little of a scholar, and so inelegant in his expressions? And yet wherein consisted the particular genius of these men, so entirely opposite to one another, if it was not, principally, in the perfect knowledge which truly intuitively they possessed of human character?

"In the same manner it has been said of General Jackson that he is incapable of writing a good English sentence, as if this were the standard by which to measure the capacity of a political chief, especially in America, where, out of a hundred senators and representatives, scarcely one has received what in Europe would be called a literary education. If classical learning were to constitute the scale by which to measure the talents of our statesmen, how far would they not rank behind the paltriest Prussian schoolmaster! General Jackson understood the people of the United States better than, perhaps, any President before him, and developed as much energy in his administration as any American statesman. I do not here speak as a partisan, nor do I wish to inquire whether all his measures were beneficial to the people; but they were, at least, all in unison with his political doctrines, and carried through with an iron consequence, notwithstanding the enormous opposition that wealth, and, in a great degree, also talent, put in the way of their execution. And yet they call Jackson a second-rate man, because he is not a regular *speechifyer*, or has never published a long article in the newspapers!

"To judge of a man like General Jackson, one must not analyze him after the manner of a chemist; one must not separate his talents—his oratory—his style of composition—his generalship, &c.; but take the *tout ensemble* of the man, and I venture to say there is not such another in the United States. It is useless to draw envious comparisons between him and Washington, Wellington, Napoleon, Jefferson, and so forth. Great men always wear the imprints of the times and circumstances which call their talents into action; but history is sure to preserve the name of any man who has had the strength and genius to stamp his own character on the people over whose destinies he presided. General Jackson has many political enemies, and his political doctrines are perhaps only maintained— I will not say maintainable—by his own great personality. His successor in office may not be able to continue to make head against the opposition—another

party may get into power, and introduce different doctrines into the administration of the country—but the impulse which General Jackson has given to the democracy of America will always continue to be felt, and impel the government in a more or less popular direction."

"You are a great friend of General Jackson," said I, "from the animated defense you make of his character."

"I certainly am, sir," said he; "and I do not know a single man of our party that is not warmly attached to him. Not that I approve of all his political principles; but I like the man, and would rather see *him* President than any other."

"You have spoken my very heart," cried the other senator. "I like *Old Hickory*, because he is just the man for the people, and as immovable as a rock. One always knows where to find him."

"He is just the man our party wanted," rejoined the first senator, "in order to take the lead."

"And I like Old Ironhead," said the member, "because he is a man after my own sort. When he once says he is your friend, he *is* your friend; but once your enemy, then *look out for breakers*."

"And, what is more," interrupted the senator, "his hatred is of that pure Saxon kind which is always coupled with moral horror; and, for that reason, irreconcilable."

"And, what is better than all," cried the member, chuckling, "he has a good memory; he never forgets a man who has rendered him a service, nor does he ever cease to remember an injury. The former is sure of being rewarded; the latter will with difficulty escape punishment. Mr. Adams, during his Presidency, was pusillanimous enough to endeavour to reconcile his enemies by all sorts of *douceurs;* he appointed them to office, invited them to dinner, and distinguished them even before his friends. This conduct naturally alienated the latter; while the former, perceiving his drift, did not think themselves bound to be grateful for his attentions. General Jackson introduced the doctrine of reward and punishment, and has '*got along*' with it much better than his warmest friends anticipated. He appointed his friends to office, and dismissed his antagonists the moment they had taken an active part in politics. That principle, sir, is the proper one to go upon. The hope of reward, and the fear of punishment, govern men in politics and religion." ...

II. THE PERSPECTIVES OF TWENTIETH-CENTURY HISTORIANS

Frederick Jackson Turner: JACKSONIAN DEMOCRACY

Frederick Jackson Turner is firmly established as a major figure in American historiography because of his writings on the significance of the frontier in American history. Indeed, his provocative essays on the frontier in American history gave birth to a "frontier school" among historical writers in the early decades of the twentieth century. In the years before his death in 1932, Turner labored to apply his system of historical explanation to the very difficult period of American history between 1830 and 1850. Through the devoted efforts of his friends, Turner's painstaking ecological analyses in this period were published in a book entitled, The United States, 1830–1850: The Nation and Its Sections. *The selection which follows demonstrates how he sought to relate Jacksonian democracy to the traits of frontier society.*

PRIOR to 1830 the larger part of the interior of the Union had been colonized from the back country of the South Atlantic section. It was not the tidewater planter who furnished the mass of these settlers, but the nonslaveholding upcountry farmer of the Piedmont region. In an earlier generation, these uplands had been settled by a combined stream of Scotch-Irish and Germans from Pennsylvania and by the yeoman pioneers who had pressed forward the Virginia and Carolina frontiers. Mingled with them were the gentry, but these were far outnumbered by the pioneers, with ax and rifle, who crossed the mountains and cut out new homes on the "Western Waters."

By 1830 they gave the tone to the society of a vast region stretching west from the Appalachian system and including, with some exceptions, the southern counties of Ohio, Indiana, and Illinois, north of the Ohio River, and all the rest of the West to the Gulf of Mexico. Over most of Pennsylvania and interior Virginia and North Carolina, the same type was preponderant.

The ideas and the leaders of this interior-valley society were profoundly to influence the political issues of the nation in the interval between the loss of power by the Old Dominion and the seizure of control by the Cotton Kingdom.

In the period of the Revolution, the "men of the Western Waters" or "men of the Western World," as they called themselves, had forced their way into the Ohio and Tennessee valleys through the passes of the Allegheny Mountains, and in the years that followed they steadily increased their numbers and their power. Thus, the Mississippi Valley of 1830 became the home of forest pioneers. These

Reprinted by permission from Frederick Jackson Turner, *The United States, 1830–1850* (New York, Holt, Rinehart & Winston, Inc., 1935), pp. 18–28.

men, shut off by the mountains from the coast, were the first Americans to break decisively with the Europeans, and to a large extent with the tidewater people.

Composed of various stocks, the special element of Andrew Jackson's people was the Scotch-Irish—the contentious Calvinistic advocates of liberty. Wherever the Calvinist went, he fought arbitrary rule and substituted the doctrine of government by covenant—the free consent of the governed people. Of the Calvinists, none were more strenuous in insistence upon these ideas than the North-of-Ireland folk who came to America. Along with them were the descendants of the English-speaking colonists who had moved away from conventional society to the frontier, and German settlers who in the course of the eighteenth century had drifted from Pennsylvania into the back country of the southern colonies. The Scotch-Irish had been accustomed to the life of cattle-raisers and fighters. The Germans brought with them less of the militant spirit and more of a thrifty, balanced agricultural life. The backwoods families made their ten- or twenty-acre clearing in the surrounding forest with the woodsman's tool, the American ax. They developed an individualism and with it a certain narrowness of view, and emphasized the doctrine of equality. Land was almost free, for, when the pioneer could not purchase, he could settle in his clearing as a squatter and either find the means for paying for it by his later crops or sell his improvements and pass on to a new region, for he was pre-eminently "on the move." His "neighbor's smoke vexed his eyes"; long before the bark began to dry upon his fence rails, he felt the call to new clearings.

He did not raise extensive crops for a market, but primarily for the subsistence of his family, and he lived to a large extent upon the "hog and hominy" furnished by the swine which fed upon the acorns about the clearing and the corn which made his earliest and chief crop. He had few or no grist- or saw-mills and his log house was the center of a simple and primitive life.

Along with individualism, self-reliance, and equality, went antagonism to the restraints of government. His own gun defended him. Population was sparse and there was no multitude of jostling interests, such as accompanied dense settlement and required a complicated system of government. There were no intricate business relations to need the intervention of the law. Society itself seemed to have dissolved into its individual atoms, at the same time that tradition, precedent—in a word, the past—lost its power by this migration into the new world beyond the mountains.

It was not only a society in which the love of equality was prominent: it was also a competitive society. To its socialist critics it has seemed not so much a democracy as a society whose members were "expectant capitalists." And this, indeed, is a part of its character. It was based upon the idea of the fair chance for all men, not on the conception of leveling by arbitrary methods and especially by law. But, while this is true, it must also be remembered that the simplicity of life in this region and these years, together with the vast extent of unoccupied land and unexploited resources, made it easy for this upcountry democrat to conceive of equality and competitive individualism as consistent elements of democracy. Just in proportion as competition increased, new fields for activity opened and artificial inequalities were checked. The self-made man was the ideal of this society.

As a part of the same conditions, men readily took the law into their own hands. A crime was more a personal affront to the victim than an outrage upon the law of the land. Substantial justice secured in the most direct way was its aim. It had little patience with fine-drawn legal or constitutional distinctions, or even scruples of method. If the thing was in itself proper to be done, then the most immediate, rough-and-ready, effective way was the best way.

From the first, it was evident that these men had means of supplementing their individual activity by informal combinations. One of the things that impressed all early travelers in the United States was the capacity for extra-legal association. This was natural enough, for in America we can study the process by which social customs form and crystallize into law. We can even see how the personal leader becomes the governmental official. This power of the pioneers to join together for a common end, without the intervention of governmental institutions, was one of their marked characteristics. The logrolling, the house raising, the husking bee, the apple paring, the squatters' associations whereby they protected themselves against the speculators in securing title to their clearings on the public domain, the camp meeting, and the courts of "Judge Lynch," are a few of the indications of this attitude.

It is well to emphasize this American trait, because in a modified way it has come to be one of the most characteristic and important features of the United States of today. America does, through informal association and understandings on the part of the people, many of the things which in the Old World are and can be done only by governmental intervention and compulsion. The actions of these associations had an authority akin to that of law. They were usually, not so much evidences of a disrespect for law and order, as the only means by which real law and order were possible in a region where settlement and society had gone in advance of the institutions and instrumentalities of organized society.

Because of these elements of individualistic competition and the power of spontaneous association, leadership, based upon the qualities most serviceable to this young society, easily developed. In the first generation of these pioneers, military companies chose their own officers, each palisaded village had its own natural commander, every community had its hero. And these local leaders, good haters and firm friends, were, like the chiefs whom Tacitus describes, bound to reward their followers. After the War of 1812, Andrew Jackson became the hero of the Mississippi Valley and of the democracy of the less densely settled regions in general.

If we add to these aspects of backwoods democracy its spiritual qualities, we shall more easily understand the significance of the background of Jackson. These men were emotional. As they wrested their clearings from the woods and from the savages who surrounded them, as they expanded those clearings and saw the beginnings of commonwealths where only little communities had been, and as they saw these commonwealths touch hands with each other along the great course of the Mississippi River, they became enthusiastically optimistic and confident of the continued expansion of this democracy. They had faith in themselves and their destiny. And that optimistic faith, that belief in the worth and possibility of the common man, was responsible both for their confidence in their own ability to rule and for their passion for expansion. They looked to the future. "Others appeal to history: an American appeals to prophecy; and with Malthus in one hand and a map of the back country in the other, he boldly defies us to a comparison with America as she is to be," said a London periodical in 1821. They made of their task almost a religion. Just because, perhaps, of the usual isolation of their lives, when they came together in associations —whether of the camp meeting or of the political gathering—they felt the influence of a common emotion and enthusiasm. Lord Bryce aptly said that the southern-upland folk have a "high religious voltage." Whether Scotch-Irish Presbyterians, Baptists, or Methodists, these people saturated their religion and their politics with emotion. Both the stump and the pulpit were centers of dynamic energy, electric cells capable of starting far-flowing currents. These men *felt* both their religion and their democracy. They were not tolerant of "new-fangled" doctrines.

This democracy was one that involved a real feeling of social comradeship among its widespread members. Justice Catron, who came from Tennessee to the Supreme Court in the Presidency of Jackson, said: "The people of New Orleans and St. Louis are next neighbours. . . . if we desire to know any thing [about] a man in any quarter of the Union, we enquire of our next neighbour, who but the other day lived by him." Exaggerated as this is, it nevertheless had a surprising measure of truth. For the Mississippi River was the great highway down which groups of pioneers like Abraham Lincoln, on their rafts and flatboats, brought the little neighborhood surplus. After the steamboat came to the Western Waters,

the voyages up and down, by merchants and by farmers shifting their homes, brought people into contact with each other over wide areas.

All of southern Indiana and southern Illinois, together with Missouri, Arkansas, and the northern parts of Mississippi and Alabama, were but the periphery of the expanding upcountry society which found its center in Kentucky and Tennessee. This enlarged neighborhood democracy was determined, not by a reluctant admission that under the law one man was as good as another: it was based upon a "genuine feeling of good fellowship," sympathy, and understanding. This was important in the region into which so many different commonwealths were pouring their populations. It was by no means the case that these men lost their prejudices: they had the universal antipathies for different customs and different regions. But the very newness of their society made these prejudices less obstinate than in older sections. Therefore, the Mississippi Valley was the region in which the process of mixture of peoples, ideas, and institutions was most easily effected.

This meant nationalism as well as friendly intercourse. Communities were too new and varied in their composition to have the historical state-feeling of the Old Thirteen. All of their experiences, moreover, tended to make them appeal to the general government for protection and advantages. This government was too remote to lay much restraint upon daily life; at the same time, it was able to furnish them the backing for their designs of building up this region into which the nation was expanding.

De Tocqueville, early in the thirties, wrote:

To evade the bondage of system and

habit, of family-maxims, class-opinions, and, in some degree, of national prejudices; to accept tradition only as a means of information, and existing facts only as a lesson to be used in doing otherwise and doing better; to seek the reason of things for one's self, and in one's self alone; to tend to results without being bound to means, and to aim at the substance through the form;—such are the principal characteristics of what I shall call the philosophical method of the Americans.

But if I go further, and seek amongst these characteristics the principal one which includes almost all the rest, I discover that, in most of the operations of mind, each American appeals only to the individual effort of his own understanding.

De Tocqueville was, in fact, describing American pioneer democracy in the days of Jackson. But the best expression of frontier democracy which I have ever seen is in the petition of the frank, rude frontiersmen of western Virginia, at the close of the Revolution, in their demand for statehood separate from the Old Dominion:

Some of our fellow citizens may think we are not yet able to conduct our affairs, and consult our interest; but if our society is rude, much wisdom is not necessary to supply our wants, and a fool can sometimes put on his clothes better than a wise man can do it for him. We are not against hearing council; but we attend more to our own feelings than to the argumentation of others.

They add that the whole authority of the state rests ultimately upon the opinions and judgments of men who are generally as void of experience as themselves. This is the authentic voice of his people at the time when Andrew Jackson, of Tennessee, won the Presidency. And, because of the large proportion of the country that had recently undergone frontier conditions or was still on the frontier, it was at that time also the voice of the average American democrat.

In order to understand the means by which this leader, trained on the frontier, expressing its militant quality and its democracy, won the Presidency, we must draw a distinction between the Jackson men and the Jacksonian Democrats in 1828. The "Jackson men" included, not only the trans-Allegheny followers of the "Old Hero," and the kindred people of Pennsylvania, but also the New York democracy and the tidewater aristocracy of the southern seaboard. Nevertheless, Jacksonian Democracy was based primarily upon the characteristics of the back country. Jackson was himself a product of the frontier West—that West which was born of the southern upland in the days when a sharp contrast existed between the interior farmers and the tidewater planters.

Although he grew up in this frontier society, he had become a man of property, a cotton planter, a leader who used his leadership to protect the interests of himself and conservative friends in days when all men on the frontier, in the midst of abundant opportunities, strove to build up their fortunes. He had even found himself, in Tennessee, in opposition to political groups whose policies were later to become his own. Among his earlier friends were men to whom the stigma of "Federalists" was attached. "Opportunist" in his politics, as he has been described, he was none the less the national leader to whom frontier democracy turned, who bore in his own personal experiences and qualities many of the frontiersmen's fundamental characteristics. This by no means prevented, in his own state of Tennessee, bitter factional rivalries and resentments when he gave to statesmen from other sections his confidence and his political rewards. He sometimes purchased national leadership at the cost of losing his own state.

The widening of the suffrage in the older states, by statute and by constitutional change, had been in active progress, and the newer states had, almost from their birth, reposed political power in the hands of the people, either by white manhood suffrage or by so low a tax qualification as to amount to the same thing. By 1830 there were few states that, in practice, had not come to this. The Western states had also based representation, in both houses of their legislatures, on numbers rather than on a combination of property and population. This marked a revolt, characteristic of the period, against the idea that property was entitled to a special representation, against the planter conviction, voiced by John Randolph, that the mere majority, "King Numbers," was tyrannous.

But Randolph's doctrine was ascendant in the tidewater counties of the South Atlantic States, and the terms of the Declaration of Independence which were inconsistent with the alleged primary purpose of government to protect the property-holding class, were repudiated. When, in previous years, the flood of Scotch-Irish, Germans, and other newcomers had passed into the back country from the North and had cut across the old lines of slow expansion from the eastern shores, the small counties of the tidewater refused to subdivide the large interior counties as the increased population entered them. They refused to reapportion legislative representation and to make adequate changes in the franchise to meet the changed conditions. Fearing that their historic social structure, and their political control, would be endangered and that the poor and rude but ambitious democracy of the nonslaveholding farmers of the interior would ex-

ploit the coast by taxing its property for the building of their roads, the development of their schools, and like expenditures, the tidewater planters determined that the coastal minority must retain its power. They even feared the antislavery sentiment of the western counties and their responsiveness to national, rather than to state, leadership. Gradual abolition had many friends in these countries.

Property's defense of its special privileges, by means of legislative apportionments and the limitation of the franchise, had been exhibited in the constitutional conventions of New York and Massachusetts in 1820. In Massachusetts, however, where the small towns in the interior of the state had a long established advantage in representation proportionate to population, it was the rapidly increasing urban population which sought to secure political power in proportion to its numbers. In New York the argument had been made that an enlargement of the franchise would increase the actual power of the master of industry by his control over the votes of his workmen. Thus, while the contest in the South Atlantic section was that of a Western democracy seeking adequate political recognition, in these Northern states the struggle was made by the growing coastal cities, seeking more adequate representation. In both cases there resulted regional struggles within the state.

To many Americans, Jackson's election seemed a humiliating catastrophe. John Quincy Adams refused to attend the ceremonies when Harvard bestowed the degree of Doctor of Laws upon his successor, explaining that he would not be present to witness her disgrace in conferring her highest literary honors upon a barbarian who could not write a sentence of grammar and hardly could spell his own name. Jackson's penmanship was not clerkly, his spelling was at times modern in the directness with which he reached the desired result, and the grammarian can often find flaws in his sentences. But Adams's description does injustice to the manuscripts of Jackson. The political judgment and foresight which were imperfectly clothed in orthographic garments soon make one forget these aspects.

"General Jackson's manners," said Webster in 1824, "are more presidential than those of any of the candidates. He is grave, mild, and reserved." Harriet Martineau, who visited him in the early thirties and who was sufficiently familiar with the highest English official society to be a good judge, said that he did the honors of his house with gentleness and politeness. He seemed to her "a man made to impress a very distinct idea of himself on all minds." She noted that his countenance commonly bore an expression of melancholy gravity, but from his eyes, when aroused, the fires of passion flashed and his whole person then looked formidable enough. We have a pen portrait from Thomas Hamilton, another English traveler of the time:

Tall and thin, with an erect, military bearing, and a head set with considerable *fierté* upon his shoulders. A stranger would at once pronounce upon his expression, on his frame and features, voice and action, on a natural and most peculiar warlikeness. He has, not to speak disrespectfully, a *game cock* all over him. His face is unlike any other. Its prevailing expression is energy;

but there is, so to speak, a lofty honorableness in its worn lines; his eye is of a dangerous fixedness, deep set and overhung by bushy gray eyebrows; his features long with strong, ridgy lines running through his cheeks, his forehead a good deal seamed and his white hair stiff and wirey, brushed obstinately back.

Here we perceive a man of prejudice, passion, and will, born to fight, and carrying a commission from the populace.

His triumph constituted an epoch in American history. To the late historian, Professor von Holst, it appeared the beginning of a downward path for the body politic, the rejection of the rule of the better classes, of the intelligent and well-to-do, and the substitution of the feelings and will of the masses for the organized and disciplined direction of the more efficient.

But the "reign of Andrew Jackson" is a test of men's attitude toward the problem of government. On the whole, it must be said that Jackson's Presidency was more representative of the America of his time than would have been that of any of his rivals. The instincts of the American people in supporting him conformed to the general drift of the tendencies of this New World democracy—a democracy which preferred persons to property, an active share by the people in government to the greater system and efficiency of a scientific administration by experts or by an established élite who dealt with the people from above. . . .

Arthur Meier Schlesinger, Jr.: THE AGE OF JACKSON

At the end of his career, Turner's thesis concerning the significance of the frontier in American history was under attack by historical scholars. During the 1930's, almost every aspect of the frontier hypothesis was subjected to such intensive criticism that younger historians were less disposed to use Turner's explanatory methods. Thus, when Arthur Meier Schlesinger, Jr. published his provocative and prize-winning book, The Age of Jackson, *in 1945, he explicitly disavowed much of Turner's interpretation of Jacksonian democracy. To Schlesinger, the East and not the West was "the source of the effective expression of Jacksonian radicalism, and Eastern ideas rose to supremacy in Washington as Jacksonianism changed from agitation into a program." The following selections from* The Age of Jackson *reveal some of the ways in which Schlesinger built up his pattern of interpretation.*

HARD MONEY

I

THE Bank War played an indispensable role in the precipitation of hard-money ideas. It dramatized currency questions in a way which captured the imagination of the people and excited their desire for further action of the financial front. It enlisted the enthusiasm of intellectuals, stimulating them to further analysis, widening the range and competence of economic theory. It tightened class lines, and the new bitterness of feeling sharpened the intellectual weapons.

Above all, the Bank War triumphantly established Jackson in the confidence of the people. Their faith in him had survived ordeals and won vindication: thereafter, when faced by a choice between Jackson and a cherished policy, most of them would choose Jackson. The effect of this mandate was particularly to sell the West on an intricate economic program, which many Westerners did not understand and which ran counter to their preconceptions.

The uncertainty about the West had postponed the avowal of the hard-money system. The veto message, written by three men of known hard-money convictions, Jackson, Taney, and Kendall, suppressed mention of the doctrine, as if by main force. But the election of 1832 increased Jackson's confidence. He could have lost the entire West and still have broken even with Clay, but he carried the whole West except for Kentucky. He now felt certain of vigorous national support, and also of probable Western support, even for his economic ideas. Not all the West would follow, of course, and even three leaders from his own state turned against him on the currency question: his old friend Hugh Lawson White, young and able John Bell, and the picturesque if somewhat phony frontiersman, Davy Crockett. Others of his Western supporters, like Robert J. Walker of Mississippi, were careful to disclaim any

From *The Age of Jackson,* by Arthur M. Schlesinger, Jr., by permission of Little, Brown & Co., pp. 115–131, 510–515.

hard-money leaning. But, on the whole, the magic of Jackson's name was fairly certain to win Western approval for almost anything.

He thus was emboldened to come out publicly for the hard-money policy, expressing himself first in his interview with the Philadelphia delegation a few days before his second inaugural. His objective, he said, was gradually to reduce the circulation of paper, by forbidding deposit banks to issue small notes and by refusing such notes in payment for taxes, until all notes under twenty dollars would be eliminated and "thus a metallic currency be ensured for all the common purposes of life, while the use of bank notes would be confined to those engaged in commerce."

Soon after, he reorganized his cabinet, turning it for the first time into an effective unit. McLane and Duane, both evidently hostile to a radical economic policy, were replaced by John Forsyth in the State Department and Roger B. Taney in the Treasury. William T. Barry, whose incompetence as Postmaster General finally drove even Jackson to despair, was succeeded by Amos Kendall. Benjamin F. Butler of New York, Van Buren's former law partner, followed Taney as Attorney General, and, after Taney's eventual rejection by the Senate, Levi Woodbury was promoted to the Treasury. In this circle of staunch hard-money men Lewis Cass could only relapse into mournful silence. The administration was now streamlined for action.

II

The hard-money system owed many of its maxims and dogmas to the Jeffersonians, and much of its vitality to the Northern workingmen who backed it so warmly; but the man to whom, after Jackson, Benton and Taney, it perhaps

owed most for its emergence as a constructive policy was William M. Gouge, the Philadelphia editor and economist. Gouge put the hard-money doctrines in the clearest form, furnished the most cogent indictment of the paper system, stated the general problems in a way (unlike the Jeffersonian) relevant to a society where finance capitalism was well entrenched, and proved unfailingly resourceful in working out the practical measures to realize his policy. Thirty-seven years old in 1833, he had been from 1823 to 1831 editor and part proprietor of the *Philadelphia Gazette*. For the next two years, he busied himself with a treatise on the banking system, published in Philadelphia in February, 1833, under the title *A Short History of Paper Money and Banking in the United States.*

The work consisted of an analysis of the social consequences of the paper system, followed by a detailed account of the history of paper money in America. The first section set forth the broad theoretical case, while the second provided the crushing documentation. Facts were Gouge's most powerful weapons; and in a plain, circumstantial way, occasionally flavored by irony, constantly buttressed by names, dates and citations, he supplied a crisp and comprehensive statement of the hard-money position.

The book became an instant success. Probably no work in economics had ever circulated so widely in the United States. The first edition was nearly exhausted by the fall of 1834, and, in 1835, it was reprinted in cheap stereotyped form to sell for twenty-five cents. By 1837 it had gone into a third edition. It was serialized in the *New York Evening Post* in 1834, and later in the *Washington Globe* and many other papers. William Cobbett published an English edition, and an abridged version was translated into French and printed at Brussels. All the radicals of the day read it voraciously—William Leggett, Theophilus Fisk, Orestes A. Brownson, William Cullen Bryant—and paid cordial tribute to the author. It delighted Frank Blair, was passed from hand to hand in the inner circle of the government; and early in 1835 Gouge was called down to Washington to take a job under Levi Woodbury in the Treasury Department. There his terse and hard-hitting memoranda were to exert for many years an important influence on financial policy.

The book's success was deserved. Its historical sections went unchallenged, even by the most ardent defenders of the system; and Gouge's keenness of analysis, as well as his accuracy, has won the approval of our ablest historians of banking. When it was first published Condy Raguet called it "decidedly the best work on Banking that we have ever met with." Modern students have treated it with similar respect. As William Graham Sumner, no friend of Jacksonian democracy, put it, Gouge "studied this system [of paper money] in its operation more thoroughly and with more intelligence than anybody else." A popular jingle expressed contemporary appreciation:—

Of modern books, the best I know—
   The author all the world is thanking—
One written more for use than show,
   Is quaintly titled, "*Gouge* on Banking."

But still improvements might be made,
   Whilst books on books the world is scrouging,
Let *Biddle* try to help the trade,
   And write one titled, "Banks on *Gouging*."

III

The hard-money policy was conceived by Gouge and its other champions as a total alternative to the Hamiltonian system. Its central point was the exclusion of banks from control over the currency. It was not, as its opponents persisted in describing it, a demand for the annihilation of the banking system and the establishment of an exclusively metallic currency. It proposed merely to limit bank paper to commercial transactions, and to confine banks to the functions of deposit and discount, slowly withdrawing from them the privilege of note issue.

The main purposes were three. One was essentially economic: to prevent periodic depressions; another essentially political: to prevent the rise within the state of independent powers, not responsible to the people and able to defy the government; and the third essentially social: to prevent the rule of a moneyed aristocracy systematically exploiting the "humble members of society."

The economic argument was brought to public attention largely by Benton and Gouge, and it drew somewhat on the reports of the English bullionists. The political was, of course, central in the American tradition; it was perhaps the particular contribution of the frontier to this controversy, and had been thrust forward during the Kentucky Relief War. The social argument represented the Jeffersonian legacy and was indebted considerably in its details to John Taylor of Caroline. As political expediency dictated, one could be stressed at certain times and others concealed. The Bank veto, for example, confined itself mainly to the second argument, with some suggestions of the third. But, after the election of 1832 had demonstrated the national confidence in Jackson, the administration began to urge all three. Gouge's book stated them conveniently, and Jackson's Farewell Address provided an excellent brief summary.

The economic argument turned ultimately on varying attitudes toward the concrete economy as an environment for living, rather than on disagreement over abstract principles. Alexander Hamilton in his eagerness to make out a case for paper money had once argued that note issue constituted "an absolute increase of capital," but this obviously untenable view was pretty well abandoned by 1830. Even the most fervent admirers of paper money acknowledged the value of increasing the proportion of specie in the circulating medium. Nicholas Biddle himself in some moods was a hard-money man. Daniel Webster loudly and constantly proclaimed the evils of overissue, except when he had to vote on a measure intended to prevent it.

Yet men like Biddle and Webster plainly preferred in last analysis a speculative economy, with quick expansion, huge gains and huge risks. During the investigation of the Bank by the Clayton Committee, when Cambreleng asked whether the existing banking system did not encourage speculation, Biddle replied: "Until the nature of man is changed, men will become speculators and bankrupts—under any system—and I do not perceive that our own is specially calculated to create them." Cambreleng became more specific. Would not the system be more healthy if note issue were forbidden? Biddle hedged: "I fear I do not comprehend all this. . . . That banks do occasional mischief there can be no doubt; but until some valuable improvement is found which supplies unmixed good, this is no objection to them. And constituted as they now are, the banks of the United States may be considered safe instruments of commerce."

Biddle and men like him were willing to take the chance of depression in exchange for the thrills and opportunities of boom. But others confronted a specula-

tive situation with much less confidence. Men of small and fairly fixed income—farmers, laborers, mechanics, petty shopkeepers, many of the Southern planters —felt themselves the victims of baffling and malevolent economic forces which they could not profit by or control.

On the most obvious level, the working classes believed that they were regularly cheated by paper money. A good portion of the small notes they received in wages were depreciated, worthless or conterfeit. Unscrupulous employers even bought up depreciated notes and palmed them off on their workingmen at face value. And, in the larger economic picture, all the stable-income classes had to stand by helpless and impotent during the unpredictable rise and fall of prices or ebb and flow of credit. Their reaction to a gambling economy was not delight at the opening up of chances for gain, but an intense feeling of insecurity. Jackson expressed their pent-up exasperation in his exclamation to the Baltimore committee on stock-jobbers, brokers and gamblers—"would to God, they were all swept from the land!"

The administration proposed to rescue the working classes from this treacherous economic order. "It is time," declared Taney, "that the just claims of this portion of society should be regarded in our legislation in relation to the currency. So far we have been providing facilities for those employed in extensive commerce, and have left the mechanic and the laborer to all the hazards of an insecure and unstable circulating medium." Jackson pronounced it "the duty of every government, so to regulate its currency as to protect this numerous class, as far as practicable, from the impositions of avarice and fraud."

Prompted by these aims, the Jacksonians began to sketch out fairly coherent theories of self-generating business cycles. Condy Raguet was perhaps the first to adumbrate the general theory, and Gouge set forth the classic description in his *Paper Money*.

In its simplest outline the theory was this: Banks incline to overissue their notes. Prices then rise, and a speculative fever begins to spread. Excited by the appearance of prosperity that accompanies boom, people spend freely. The general expansion of credit leads to overtrading and inflation. Every new business operation on credit creates more promissory notes, and these increase the demand for discounts, till finally the currency depreciates so greatly that specie is required for export in order to pay foreign debts. With specie at a premium, contraction sets in. Banks call in their loans, timid people start runs on banks, contraction turns to panic, and panic to collapse. "One man is unable to pay his debts," wrote Gouge. "His creditor depended on him for the means of paying a third person to whom he is himself indebted. The circle extends through society. Multitudes become bankrupt, and a few successful speculators get possession of the earnings and savings of many of their frugal and industrious neighbors."

The more careful analysts pointed out the complex interdependence of bank credit and general business activity, but political pamphleteers skipped the subtleties and blamed depressions on the paper-money system alone. Bank paper, they argued, stimulated the original boom psychology by beguiling businessmen into overtrading at times of rising prices. It linked the whole system so intimately that the failure of one merchant might prevent a dozen others from meeting their obligations. And most particularly, the expansion or contraction of paper in circulation bore only a perverse

and futile relation to actual business needs. In the words of George Bancroft, it "expands when rising prices require a check to enterprise, and contracts when falling prices make credit most desirable." Or, as Theophilus Fisk put it with more venom, "The moment a spirit of speculation can be excited, the banks increase the flame by pouring oil upon it; the instant a reaction takes place, they add to the distress a thousand-fold."

If by modern standards highly inadequate, this currency theory of depression yet represented a considerable advance over no theory at all. Very little was then said of general overproduction as a cause of depression. Some men, like Robert Rantoul, Jr., laid special stress on the glutting of markets as a factor in crisis; but many would agree with Gouge's note on such arguments, that "if the real wants of the community, and not their ability to pay, be considered, it will not, perhaps, be found that any one useful trade or profession has too many members," and accept his emphasis on the problem of "ability to pay." In 1843 Orestes A. Brownson in a brilliant passage placed the blame squarely on "our vicious method of distributing the products of labor." "More can be produced, in any given year," he wrote, "with the present productive power, than can be sold in any given five years." The fault lies in distribution.

We create a surplus—that is a surplus, not when we consider the wants of the people, but when we consider the state of the markets—and then must slacken our hand till the surplus is worked off. During this time, while we are working off the surplus, while the mills run short time, or stop altogether, the workmen must want employment. The evil is inherent in the system.

But this line of thought evidently failed

to strike much response and was carried no farther.

IV

The political argument—opposition to the rise of independent powers within the state—had general premises deeply entrenched in the national consciousness. Everyone, from right to left, believed, with more or fewer qualifications, that sovereignty belonged to the people. It was but one step from this to declare that the people's government, therefore, should not be defied by private institutions; and it was easy to extend this proposition to economic institutions, as well as political.

In their nature as corporations, banks gave rise to one set of objections, springing from their monopoly of financial prerogative through special charter. Indeed, they provided so much the most flagrant instances of abuse of corporate privilege that they were mainly responsible for fixing national attention on the problem.

Their power over the currency was viewed as an especially grave encroachment on the domain of government. The regulation of the currency, in the words of Benton, was "one of the highest and most delicate acts of sovereign power . . . precisely equivalent to the power to create currency"; and he considered it "too great a power to be trusted to any banking company whatever, or to any authority but the highest and most responsible which was known to our form of Government." Commercial credit was another matter, "an affair of trade," as Cambreleng put it, "and not of government"; and the logic of this position pointed to the abolition of banks of note issue, on the one hand, and the establishment of free competition among banks of discount and deposit, on the other. The crucial error of the federal government, according to the hard-money advocates, lay in accepting bank notes in the payment of federal dues, by which it thus extended and virtually underwrote the credit of the banks. The remedy was to exclude bank notes from government payments.

The behavior of banks in practice, moreover, violated the national faith in popular rule. The most powerful argument against Biddle's Bank was always its calm assumption of independence. "The Bank of the United States," Jackson charged, "is in itself a Government which has gradually increased in strength from the day of its establishment. The question between it and the people has become one of power." Biddle's conduct, in 1834, in refusing to allow a House committee to investigate the Bank records or examine the Bank officers, was simply the climax of his oft-expressed theory of the Bank's independence. "This powerful corporation, and those who defend it," as Taney said, without much exaggeration, "seem to regard it as an independent sovereignty, and to have forgotten that it owes any duties to the People, or is bound by any laws but its own will."

But Biddle was simply exhibiting on a larger scale habits long established in banking experience. William Graham Sumner concisely summed up the pretensions of the banks:—

The bankers had methods of doing things which were customary and conventional, but . . . contrary both to ordinary morality and to law as applied to similar matters outside of banks. . . . The banks also disregarded law so habitually that it became a commonplace that law could not bind them. We search almost in vain through the law reports for any decisions on the rights or authority of the State over banks or the duties of banks to the State. It may be said that no attempts were made to test or enforce the right of the State against banks, and that, as a matter of practice, it had none. The banks were almost irresponsible. Such decisions as bear at all on the authority of the State over banks proceed from the attempts of the banks to resist the exercise of any authority whatever.

Such a situation obviously could not be long borne. As Theophilus Fisk put it, "Either the State is sovereign, or the Banks are."

v

The social argument—the battle against domination by "the rich and powerful"—represented the culmination of the hard-money doctrine. The economic and political arguments, though capable of standing by themselves, were ultimately directed at conditions preliminary to the question: who shall rule in the state? The recurrent economic crises were evil, not only in themselves, but because they facilitated a redistribution of wealth that built up the moneyed aristocracy. The irresponsible political sovereignties were evil, not only in themselves, but because they provided the aristocracy with instruments of power and places of refuge.

The Bank War compelled people to speculate once again about the conflict of classes. "There are but two parties," exclaimed Thomas Hart Benton, giving the period its keynote; "there never has been but two parties . . . founded in the radical question, whether PEOPLE, or PROPERTY, shall govern? Democracy implies a government by the people. . . . Aristocracy implies a government of the rich . . . and in these words are contained the sum of party distinction."

The paper banking system was considered to play a leading role in this everlasting struggle. Men living by the issue and circulation of paper money produced nothing; they added nothing to the national income; yet, they flourished and grew wealthy. Their prosperity, it was argued, must be stolen from the proceeds of productive labor—in other words, from the honest but defenseless "humble members of society"; and Gouge extensively annotated the modes of plunder.

The system was further important in the strategy of the warfare. Taney described the big Bank as "the centre, and the citadel of the moneyed power." "A national bank," declared the Massachusetts Democratic convention of 1837, "is the bulwark of the aristocracy; its outpost, and its rallying point. It is the bond of union for those who hold that Government should rest on property." To a lesser degree all banks acted as strongholds of conservatism. They provided the funds and often the initiative for combat. Their lawyers, lobbyists and newspapers were eternally active. Politicians would gather in their board rooms and consult their presidents and accept gifts of stock. More than any other kind of corporate enterprise, banks boldly intervened in politics when they felt their interests menaced.

The hard-money policy attacked both the techniques of plunder and the general strategy of warfare. By doing away with paper money, it proposed to restrict the steady transfer of wealth from the farmer and laborer to the business community. By limiting banks to commercial credit and denying them control over the currency, it proposed to lessen their influence and power. By reducing the proportion of paper money, it proposed to moderate the business cycle, and order the economy to the advantage of the worker rather than the speculator. It was a coherent policy, based on the best economic thought of the day, and formulated on a higher intellectual level than the alternatives of the opposition.

By origin and interest, it was a policy which appealed mainly to the submerged classes of the East and to the farmers of the South rather than to the frontier. Historians have too long been misled by the tableau of Jackson, the wild backwoodsman, erupting into the White House. In fact, the hard-money doctrine, which was not at all a frontier doctrine, was the controlling policy of the administration from the winter of 1833 on; and for some time it had been the secret goal of a small group, led by Jackson, Taney, Benton and Kendall, and passively encouraged by Van Buren. From the removal of the deposits to the end of Van Buren's presidency in 1840 this clique of radical Democrats sought to carry out the policy in its full implications. As soon as the hard-money program was divorced from the glamour of the Hero of New Orleans and had to rest on its inherent appeal, it did very badly in the West.

Andrew Jackson ably summed up its broad aims. "The planter, the farmer, the mechanic, and the laborer," he wrote, "all know that their success depends upon their own industry and economy, and that they must not expect to become suddenly rich by the fruits of their toil." These classes "form the great body of the people of the United States; they are the bone and sinew of the country." Yet "they are in constant danger of losing their fair influence in the Government." Why? "The mischief springs from the power which the moneyed interest derives from a paper currency, which they are able to control, from the multitude of corporations with exclusive privileges which they have succeeded in obtaining in the different States." His warning to his people was solemn. "Unless you become more watchful . . . you will in the end find that the most important powers of Government have been given or bartered away, and the control over your dearest interests has passed into the hands of these corporations."

VI

Taney and Benton worked out the details of the immediate hard-money measures. They proposed to increase the metallic basis of the currency in two directions: by the restoration of gold to circulation, and by the suppression of small notes. The first measure had been for many years close to Benton's heart. Gold had long been undervalued, at the ratio of 15 to 1, with the result that no gold eagles and only a scattering of other gold coins had been minted since 1805, and most of these rapidly left the country. Benton argued that, if the gold were not thus expelled, the amount of specie derivable from foreign commerce, added to the amount obtained from American mines, could supply all financial needs without recourse to small notes or "shinplasters." In June, 1834, his bill to revise the valuation to 16 to 1 passed Congress. As an expression of the strictly economic intentions of the hard-money policy, it made a broad appeal to all men of good will, winning the support of John Quincy Adams, Webster and Calhoun. Only diehards like Clay and Horace Binney opposed it.

The change in the coinage ratio was one of Benton's greatest triumphs. He exulted in the new flow of gold to the government mints. "This is the money the Constitution provides," he would say, "and I will not have anything to do with any other kind." Or, in another mood, "What! Do you want a coroner's jury to sit and say, 'Old Bullion died of shinplasters?'" Old Bullion was the name his hard-money fixation had won him, among his friends, at least; his enemies called him sarcastically the Gold Humbug. For a time, foes of the hard-money policy sought to ridicule Benton's reform out of existence. Gilt counters were circulated, with grotesque figures and caustic inscriptions—the "whole hog" and the "better currency." But no one dared argue directly that this infusion of specie would not improve the health of the economy.

The effects of revaluation were immediate. Levi Woodbury reported in December, 1836, that more gold had been coined in the twelve months preceding than in the first sixteen years of the mint's existence, and more in the two and a half years since revaluation than in the thirty-one before. In October, 1833, there had been only thirty million dollars of specie in the country, of which twenty-six million was in banks. In December, 1836, there was seventy-three million dollars, of which only forty-five million was in banks.

Yet the revival of gold would hardly be enough without measures to suppress small notes. This proposal had the sanction, not only of the theory of Adam Smith (and of Nicholas Biddle), but of the example of Great Britain, which had established a £5 minimum in 1829. Most economically literate conservatives acknowledged the theoretical advantages of suppression; and Congress and the Treasury, drawing on their authority to define the kind of money receivable in federal payments, could exert real, if limited, influence on the issues of state banks. A joint resolution of 1816 had made all notes from specie-paying banks acceptable in tax payments. In a Treasury circular of April, 1835, all notes under $5 were banned, and banks holding government deposits were forbidden to issue such notes. In February, 1836, a similar circular banned notes under $10, and a congressional act of April, 1836, prohibited notes under $20 after March 3, 1837, and required immediate convertibility for all notes. The conditions imposed on the deposit banks controlled their stock transactions, as well as their note issue, calling for weekly statements and ordering that they should always be open for examination. Declared Secretary Woodbury, "All mystery on the subject of banking should cease."

But these regulations had little effect on the general banking situation. Only by deliberately rousing public opinion within the states could the administration hope to abolish small notes. In some states tattered shinplasters circulated with face values of 12½ or even 6¼ cents. In December, 1834, Jackson appealed to the states to follow the national example. Pennsylvania, Maryland and Virginia already had legislation against small bills. In 1835 Maine, Connecticut and New York outlawed notes below $5, while North Carolina, Georgia, Alabama, Ohio, Indiana, and Missouri also passed restrictive measures.

VII

But the administration's campaign came too late. The wise counsels of the hard-money advocates were drowned out by the roar of the nation's greatest boom in years. The Bank of the United States alone enlarged its loans an average of two and a half million dollars a month and its paper circulation by a total of ten million dollars between December, 1834, and July, 1835. Smaller banks rushed to follow, increasing the amount of paper money from eighty-two million dollars on January 1, 1835, to one hundred and eight million, a year later, and one hundred and twenty million by December 1, 1836.

Wages climbed, opportunity seemed limitless and riches appeared to lie everywhere. A popular tract of 1836—*The Book of Wealth; in Which It Is Proved from the Bible, that It Is the Duty of Every Man to Become Rich*—suggests the temper of the day. Designed to allay any religious misgivings about joining at the trough, the book earnestly declared one thing to be certain: "no man can be obedient to God's will as revealed in the Bible, without, as the general result, becoming wealthy."

The administration watched the speculative mania with profound alarm. In the *Globe* Frank Blair repeatedly voiced the deep anxieties of the hard-money circle. "We have again and again warned the community," he wrote in the spring of 1835, "of the infatuation which had seized them since the panic, to embark in every species of extravagant speculation." A month later: "this state of things cannot last. . . . A reaction is as certain to take place as the sun is to continue its diurnal course." After a year of similar remarks: "The only remedy is to be found in banking less and trading less."

Jackson, in the early months of 1836, lifted his voice in conversation against "the mad career" in which the nation was rushing to ruin. Benton declared angrily in the Senate: "I did not join in putting down the Bank of the United States, to put up a wilderness of local banks. I did not join in putting down the paper currency of a national bank, to put up a national paper currency of a thousand local banks. I did not strike Caesar," he concluded in magnificent wrath, "to make Anthony master of Rome. . . . The present bloat in the paper system cannot continue. . . . The revulsion will come, as surely as it did in 1819–'20" When Secretary Woodbury made his report in December, 1836, he had to predict that the inflation would "produce much distress, embarrassment, and ruin, before this specie can be duly equalized, the excesses of paper sufficiently curtailed, and the exorbitant discounts gradually lessened."

A basic cause of the inflation was land speculation, and the administration had already moved to plug up this great hole in the national economy. The receivability of bank notes in payment for the public lands had practically converted the national domain into a fund for the redemption of the notes, providing in effect a capital for seven or eight hundred institutions to bank on, and filling the Treasury with more or less worthless paper. Benton had pointed out in detail how land sales passed on to the government the job of underwriting the whole banking system. Speculators would borrow five, ten, twenty, fifty thousand dollars in paper from banks on the condition of using it on the frontier. They would then pay the notes to government land offices in exchange for land, which served as security for additional loans; meanwhile, the notes circulated freely as land-office money, some never returning to the original bank for redemption, the rest only after a long interval. This racket not only subsidized the banking interest— land sales had risen from four million dollars a year to five million a quarter— but it also, in Benton's words, irretrievably entangled "the federal Government with the ups and downs of the whole paper system, and all the fluctuations, convulsions, and disasters, to which it was subject."

Benton introduced a resolution requiring that the public lands he paid for in specie. Webster, with his usual policy of supporting sound money except when concrete measures were proposed which might secure it, led the attack on this measure, and a combination of Whigs and conservative Democrats killed it in the Senate. But after adjournment Jackson had Benton draw up an executive order embodying his idea, and the famous "Specie Circular" was issued.

The business community grew furious

over this latest evidence of executive despotism. When Congress reassembled in December, the Whigs demanded the repeal of the Circular and the reopening of the land offices to wildcat money, and the Democrats split wide under the pressure. One wing, led by William Cabell Rives of Virginia and N. P. Tallmadge of New York, emerged as defenders of the state banks. Benton vainly urged the imminence of a financial explosion which would leave the Treasury holding the bag; but his efforts won him little more than denunciation as "that most miserable Jacobin of the woods of Missouri, who, with an impudence and insolence unparalleled, has attempted to overthrow the commercial and financial relations and institutions of this country." The final vote disclosed a tiny group of five men, led by Benton and Silas Wright, upholding the hard-money position. The bill passed the House and went to the President on the day before adjournment. Firm to the end, the old General returned it with his veto.

Jackson thus had to overrule Congress to sustain the hard-money position. But the Specie Circular furnished the only tense financial issue in the last years of his administration. After the panic session the great scenes of battle began to shift to the states. Here, in places inaccessible to the long arm and grim energy of General Jackson, little bands of devoted Jacksonians fought to stem the rush for bank and corporate charters, unfolding the potentialities of the Jacksonian program, enriching the techniques and amplifying the intellectual resources.

Above all, these local battles called forth the common people in cities, towns, and country—the poor day laborer, the industrious mechanic, the hard-handed farmer—the "humble members of society" everywhere. They listened for hours on hot summer days to dry expositions of financial policy. They crowded in bare and unheated halls on cold winter nights to hear about the evils of banking. They read, and thumbed, and passed along tracts and speeches attacking the paper system. They saw the dizzy climb of prices, wages lagging behind, raged silently at discounted bank notes, and wondered at the behavior of Democratic politicians pledged against voting for incorporations. They talked among themselves, with shrewdness and good sense and alarm.... Their discontent was real and widespread. It found its leaders, and the experience of these years prepared them for one great final drive on the national scene....

TRADITIONS OF DEMOCRACY

III

We have seen how the growth of impersonality in economic relations enhanced the need for the intervention of government. As the private conscience grew increasingly powerless to impose effective restraints on the methods of business, the public conscience, in the form of the democratic government, had to step in to prevent the business community from tearing society apart in its pursuit of profit. The rise of the "mass," by increasing the proportion of society only fitfully capable of making responsible decisions, added to the compulsion for state action. Yet by origin and creed the tradition of Jefferson was vigorously antistatist; and the conflict raised new problems for democratic thought.

This mistrust of government had roots deep in the American past. Many of the colonists, as Van Buren pointed out, had arrived with vivid recollections of the persecutions suffered by Puritan, Huguenot, Hussite and Dutch ancestors, which, "gradually stimulated into maturity and shape by the persevering injustice of the mother country, became political opinions of the most tenacious and enduring character." The first motive of American democracy was hostility against what was felt to be insupportable tyranny, and the war with Britain confirmed democracy in its suspicion of the state. Moreover, for people in the shadow of the Middle Ages, the history of liberty had been the history of the capture of guarantees and immunities from the state; and in the American republic itself, most interference by the central government—United States Bank, internal improvements, tariff—had been for the benefit of the business community. The instinct of democrats was thus to insist on the constitutional bounds of the state. Their experience of government and their reading of history, as Van Buren put it, destroyed all hope that "political power could be vested in remote hands, without the certainty of its being abused."

"That government is best, which governs least," "The world is too much governed"—the mottoes respectively of the *Democratic Review* and the *Washington Globe*—expressed forcibly the prevailing antigovernmental complex. The corollary was that what government was necessary should be in the hands of the states. "The man who chiefly desires to preserve the rights of the States, and he whose interests are concentrated in perpetuating the rule of the many," as the *Democratic Review* said in 1844, "must, under our political system, use the same means to attain their ends." George Bancroft observed that it was Jackson's deep conviction that "strict construction is required by the lasting welfare of the great labouring classes of the United States."

These emotions about State rights and the evil of government were absorbed into and fortified by what may be called the "Jeffersonian myth." Every great so-

cial movement, as Sorel has reminded us, generates its "social myth"—the "body of images capable of evoking instinctively all the sentiments which correspond to the different manifestations" of the movement. Such a myth, though it purports to deal with the future, is by no means to be taken as a blueprint. It "must be judged as a means of acting on the present; any attempt to discuss how far it can be taken literally as future history is devoid of sense." The myths are "not descriptions of things, but expressions of a determination to act." It is thus idle to refute a myth, since it exists as an emotional entirety whose essential function is to mobilize men for action.

Jackson in his vindication of his presidency to the Senate displayed some of the resources of the Jeffersonian myth. It had been his purpose, he said, "to heal the wounds of the Constitution and preserve it from further violation; to persuade my countrymen, so far as I may, that it is not in a splendid government supported by powerful monopolies and aristocratical establishments that they will find happiness or their liberties protection, but in a plain system, void of pomp, protecting all and granting favors to none, dispensing its blessings, like the dews of Heaven, unseen and unfelt save in the freshness and beauty they contribute to produce." The imagery discloses the underlying pattern: the Constitution undefiled vs. the Constitution violated; plain government vs. splendid government; equal rights vs. powerful monopolies; the dews of heaven, in freshness and beauty, vs. "aristocratical establishments," with their suggestions of monarchy, wealth and decadence.

The Jeffersonian myth thus implanted and sustained in the minds of its followers a whole set of social choices: simplicity vs. ostentation; frugality vs. extravagance; rectitude vs. laxity; moderation vs.

luxury; country vs. city; virtuous farmer or mechanic vs. depraved capitalist or demoralized day laborer; plain homely government vs. sumptuous complicated government; economy vs. debt; strict construction vs. loose construction; State rights vs. huge federal power; decentralization vs. concentration; democracy vs. aristocracy; purity vs. corruption.

This body of values and images animated and deepened the appeals of Jefferson, John Taylor, Jackson, Van Buren and the other Jeffersonians. They were operating in terms of a great common vision, strong, simple and satisfying, evoking the emotions which hope, memory or experience had endeared to millions of Americans, and thrusting in sharp and ugly relief the invading armies of industrialism and aristocracy. The existence of this myth in the background of the mind gave its component parts—not least the belief in the evil of government—a strong and almost sacred status.

IV

Yet change brought a growing divergence between the myth and the actuality. We have seen how the past contrasts between country and city, honest farmer and demoralized laborer, were tripped up by the realities of Jacksonian politics. In the realm of government the divergence became acute with respect to the antigovernmental complex. The neat formulas of antistatism simply failed to work. Invented as protective doctrines against aristocratic despotism, they became an embarrassment when the radical party got into power itself. Jefferson ignored them when he felt strong executive action to be necessary, and in the quiet of his retirement he even developed a general rationale for overstepping the Jeffersonian limitations.

The administration of Jackson accentuated the complexities which underlay

the deceptively simple maxims of the *Globe* and the *Democratic Review.* Granted that competition free from government intervention constituted the ideal economy, what was the Jeffersonian obligation when that freedom resulted in the growth of monopolies which destroyed competition? The Jacksonian answer was government intervention—to restore the conditions of competition; that is, to "heal the wounds of the Constitution" and re-establish the principles of government in their original purity. As John L. O'Sullivan put it, "A good deal of positive government may be yet wanted to undo the manifold mischiefs of past mis-government." Thus, the Jacksonians, under the banner of antistatism, could carry on a vigorous program of government intervention, and Jackson, ruling in the name of weak government, ended up by leaving the presidency stronger than it had ever been before.

Some of the details of the Jacksonian policy, however, caused orthodox Jeffersonians distinct discomfort, even those who managed to swallow such deviations as the Nullification Proclamation or the removal of the deposits.

The struggle to reconcile the Jeffersonian myth and the Jacksonian fact was fought out most candidly in the pages of the *Democratic Review.* The first issue contained a glowing and trustful statement of the Jeffersonian position, with the theory of weak government imbedded as the keystone. But what was the status of this theory in face of an army of corporations hostile to democracy? O'Sullivan wrestled with this difficulty in a casuistical article in the second number, eventually confining the theory to the federal government alone and vehemently attacking the Supreme Court for limiting the power of state governments over business.

But was this much help? After the

banks suspended in May, 1837, a trade-union meeting in Philadelphia had declared in a typical outburst, "On the question of the currency, we have no confidence in the State administrations generally. . . . we hereby call upon the national administration to take all such measures as it shall judge the most expedient." Where did this leave O'Sullivan's revised theory? He perceived the difficulty, and the third number carried a somewhat embarrassed article justifying the robustness of Jackson's presidency, but hoping devoutly that "those great powers resident in the Executive arm, may never again be called forth into activity."

And so it went. Jeffersonian fundamentalists got off the bandwagon early. Even a Jacksonian like Orestes A. Brownson could in certain moods exclaim with alarm at Jackson's "tendency to Centralization and his evident leaning to *Bureaucraticy*. . . . We are making more rapid strides towards . . . Centralization and to the Bureaucratic system than even the most sensitive nullifier has yet suspected."

It is no wonder that the attempt to defend Jacksonianism in terms of that government being best which governed least excited only the derision of the Whigs. To them Jacksonian policy consisted simply, as Caleb Cushing described it, of "the meddlesome interference of General Jackson in the business of the country, his prurient tampering with the currency under the pretext of reforming it," and so on. The talk about restoring constitutional purity seemed a cynical pretext for reckless government intervention.

The vital point underlying this bandying of accusations is that "intervention" is not an absolute. It is always a question of whose ox is gored. Government *must*

act; it cannot rest in Olympian impartiality. Even "governing least" is likely to be government for the benefit of the strongest group in the community. The crucial question is not, Is there "too much" government? but, Does the government promote "too much" the interests of a single group? In liberal capitalist society this question has ordinarily become in practice, Is the government serving the interests of the business community to the detriment of the nation as a whole? This has been the irrepressible conflict of capitalism: the struggle on the part of the business community to dominate the state, and on the part of the rest of society, under the leadership of "liberals," to check the political ambitions of business.

The real issue between the Whigs and Jackson was, thus, not freedom of enterprise. Both parties would concede that enterprise should be free, would claim always to be acting to protect this freedom, and each, when in possession of the state, would unhesitatingly intervene in business, on its own behalf and in the name of "freedom," by destroying United States Banks or establishing protective tariffs. The champions of Jeffersonianism were eager for government to suppress small notes and institute a ten-hour day, while the Hamiltonians would flourish free-trade principles when questions of trade-unionism or corporation control were brought up. If the men of the thirties and forties really had accepted the antistatist maxims they constantly invoked, they would not have been in political parties at all, but in lonely huts around country ponds like the one man of the day who believed radically that that government was best which governed least.

The question was not principles but power: was a "liberal" government, in fact, strong enough to act contrary to the wishes of the business community? And in the struggle over this basic question conservatism or liberalism would adopt any myth, and has adopted most which promised to promote its cause. This is not to impugn the honesty of belief in the visions excited by the myth, for no great social movement can exist without such stimulus and support. The myth, it should never be forgotten, expresses only the "determination to act." The ends of action lie necessarily in an inscrutable future.

Richard Hofstadter: ANDREW JACKSON AND THE RISE OF LIBERAL CAPITALISM

Richard Hofstadter belongs to that generation of historians that came of age during the middle thirties. His work as a historian has paralleled the growth in prestige and in effectiveness of the newer social sciences such as cultural anthropology, sociology, and social psychology. Much of his writing reflects his contacts with the literature of the social sciences. In particular, he has been concerned to explore the relationship between ideas and social situations in such books as Social Darwinism in American Thought, The American Political Tradition, *and* The Age of Reform. *The following selection is a good example of the way in which Hofstadter investigates the links between ideas and social situations. In this case, it leads him to associate Jackson more strongly with the psychology and aspirations of the "expectant capitalist" than of the Western frontiersman or the eastern workingman.*

II

THE rise of Andrew Jackson marked a new turn in the development of American political institutions. During the period from 1812 to 1828 the two-party system disappeared and personal, local, and sectional conflicts replaced broad differences over public policy as the central fact in national politics. As the presidency declined from its heights under the leadership of Washington and Jefferson, the contest for the presidential seat resolved into a scramble of local and sectional princelings for the position of heir apparent. The Virginia dynasty's practice of elevating the forthcoming president through the vice-presidency or cabinet seemed to have become a set pattern. Presidential nominations, made by party caucuses in Congress, were remote from the popular will, and since the elections of 1816 and 1820 were virtually uncontested, nomination by "King Caucus" was equivalent to being chosen president. Since the days of Jefferson there had been no major turnover in the staff of officeholders, whose members were becoming encrusted in their posts.

However, the people, the propertyless masses, were beginning, at first quietly and almost unobtrusively, to enter politics. Between 1812 and 1821 six

Reprinted from *The American Political Tradition and the Men Who Made It* by Richard Hofstadter by permission of Alfred A. Knopf, Inc. Copyright 1948, pp. 48–66.

western states entered the Union with constitutions providing for universal white manhood suffrage or a close approximation, and between 1810 and 1821 four of the older states substantially dropped property qualifications for voters. As poor farmers and workers gained the ballot, there developed a type of politician that had existed only in embryo in the Jeffersonian period—the technician of mass leadership, the caterer to mass sentiment; it was a coterie of such men in all parts of the country that converged upon the prominent figure of Jackson between 1815 and 1824. Generally subordinated in the political corporations and remote from the choicest spoils, these leaders encouraged the common feeling that popular will should control the choice of public officers and the formation of public policy. They directed popular resentment of closed political corporations against the caucus system, which they branded as a flagrant usurpation of the rights of the people, and spread the conviction that politics and administration must be taken from the hands of a social elite or a body of bureaucratic specialists and opened to mass participation. Success through politics, it was implied, must become a legitimate aspiration of the many. Jackson expressed the philosophy of this movement in his first annual message to Congress, December, 1829, when he confidently asserted:

The duties of all public offices are, or at least admit of being made, so plain and simple that men of intelligence may readily qualify themselves for their performance, and I can not but believe that more is lost by the long continuance of men in office than is generally to be gained by their experience. . . . In a country where offices are created solely for the benefit of the people no one man has any more intrinsic right to official station than another.

Rotation in office, he concluded, constituted a "leading principle in the Republican creed."

The trend toward popular activity in politics was heightened by the panic of 1819, which set class against class for the first time since the Jeffersonian era. A result of rapid expansion, speculation, and wildcat banking, the panic and ensuing depression fell heavily upon all parts of the country, but especially upon the South and West, where men had thrown all their resources into reckless buying of land. The banks, which had grossly overextended themselves, were forced to press their debtors to the wall, and through the process of foreclosure the national bank particularly became a great absentee owner of Western and Southern property. "All the flourishing cities of the West," complained Thomas Hart Benton, "are mortgaged to this money power. They may be devoured by it at any moment. They are in the jaws of the monster!" This alien power was resented with particular intensity in the West, where, as the New York *American* put it, "a wild son of Tennessee who has been with Jackson could ill brook that his bit of land, perhaps his rifle, should be torn from him by a neighboring shopkeeper, that the proceeds may travel eastward, where the 'sceptre' of money has fixed itself." The panic brought a cruel awakening for thousands who had hoped to become rich. John C. Calhoun, talking with John Quincy Adams in the spring of 1820, observed that the last two years had produced "an immense revolution of fortunes in every part of the Union, enormous multitudes in deep distress, and a general mass of disaffection to the Government not concentrated in any particular direction, but ready to seize upon any event and looking out anywhere for a leader."

Calhoun's "general mass of disaffection" was not sufficiently concentrated to prevent the re-election, unopposed, of President Monroe in 1820 in the absence of a national opposition party; but it soon transformed politics in many states. Debtors rushed into politics to defend themselves, and secured moratoriums and relief laws from the legislatures of several Western states. State legislatures, under pressure from local banking interests, waged tax wars against the Bank of the United States. A popular demand arose for laws to prevent imprisonment for debt, for a national bankruptcy law, and for new tariff and public-land policies. For the first time many Americans thought of politics as having an intimate relation to their welfare. Against this background Jackson's star rose. But, curiously, the beneficiary of this movement not only failed to encourage it, but even disapproved. The story of his evolution as a national democratic leader is a strange paradox.

North Carolina, the scene of Jackson's childhood, had been a Jeffersonian stronghold, and Jackson was nurtured on Jeffersonian ideas. In 1796 and 1800 the young Tennessean voted for the sage of Monticello. Except for his nationalism, Jackson's politics chiefly resembled agrarian Republicanism of the old school, which was opposed to banks, public debts, paper money, high tariffs, and federal internal improvements. When the Burr trial and Jefferson's pacificism disillusioned him with Jefferson, Jackson did not become a convert to Federalism but rather adhered to the Randolph-Macon school of intransigent Republicans.

Jackson's personal affairs shed much light on his ambiguous political evolution from 1796 to 1828. An event of 1796 that had a disastrous effect on his fortunes may have sown in him the seeds of that keen dislike of the Eastern money power and "paper system" which flowered during his presidency. Jackson had gone to Philadelphia to sell several thousand acres of land to a rich merchant and speculator, David Allison; he accepted notes from Allison, which he endorsed and promptly used to pay for supplies he planned to use in opening a general-merchandise store in Nashville. Allison failed, and defaulted on his notes; Jackson became liable. In order to pay the notes as they fell due, he was forced to retrench, give up the estate on which he lived, move to a smaller one built of logs, and sell many of his slaves. Subsequently his store enterprise turned out badly and he was obliged to sell out to his partners. Jackson seems never to have whined about his misfortune, but he lived for nineteen years in its shadow, remaining in debt from 1796 to 1815, when at last his military pay and allowances brought him into the clear. In the fall of 1815 he had a cash balance of over twenty-two thousand dollars at the Nashville bank, was again heavily committed in land speculations, and was building the fine new estate that has become famous as the Hermitage. Just at this time, when he was so vulnerable, the panic of 1819 struck.

The general distress of Tennessee debtors led, as in many other places, to a movement for relief. Felix Grundy, elected to the state Senate on a "relief" platform, brought forth a proposal to establish a state loan office to help debtors out of the state treasury. Creditors who refused to accept notes of the loan bank in payment of debts would have their collections suspended for two years. Jackson's own obligations forced him to press his debtors hard, and he instituted a single lawsuit against one hundred and twenty-nine of them at once. One of the few men in middle Tennessee to stand against Grudy's relief program, he sent a protest to the state legislature, which was rejected on the ground that its language was disrespectful. Having learned from the Allison episode to feel for the luckless entrepreneur, Jackson was now learning to see things from the standpoint of the local moneyed class. The emergence of class conflict in Tennessee found him squarely on the side of the haves. In 1821, when General William Carroll ran for the governorship of the state on a democratic economic program, Jackson supported Carroll's opponent, Colonel Edward Ward, a wealthy planter who had joined Jackson in fighting Grundy's scheme. Carroll was elected, and proceeded to put through a program of tax revision and constitutional and humanitarian reform, which has many elements of what historians call "Jacksonian" democracy. At the moment when Jackson was pitting himself against Carroll in Tennessee, his friends were bringing him forward as a presidential candidate. None of this prevented Grundy and Carroll from later joining the Jackson bandwagon.

Had Jackson's record on popular economic reform been a matter of primary importance, he might never have been President. But by 1824, when he first accepted a presidential nomination, prosperity had returned, hostility to banks and creditors had abated, and breaking up established political machines seemed more important to the parvenu politician and the common citizen. As chief "issues" of the campaign the caucus system shared honors with the defense of New Orleans. An outsider to the Congressional machines, a man of humble birth whose popularity was based on military achievement and whose attitude toward economic questions was unknown and of lit-

tle interest to the average voter, Jackson had a considerable edge with the new electorate.

The consequences of the campaign of 1824 settled all doubt in Jackson's mind about the presidency. Far stronger in the popular vote than any of his three rivals, John Quincy Adams, Clay, and Crawford, he still fell short of the necessary majority in the electoral college, and the election was thrown into the House of Representatives. There the position of Clay became decisive, and Clay threw his support to Adams. Subsequently, when President Adams named Clay his Secretary of State, a bitter cry went up from the Jackson following. Jackson himself was easily persuaded that Clay and Adams had been guilty of a "corrupt bargain" and determined to retake from Adams what he felt was rightfully his. The campaign of 1828 began almost immediately with Adams's administration. For four years the President, a man of monumental rectitude but a career politician of the dying order par excellence, was hounded by the corrupt-bargain charge and subjected by the Jackson professionals to a skillful campaign of vilification, which culminated in the election of 1828. In Jackson's second presidential campaign the bank was hardly mentioned. The tariff was played for what it was worth where men cared especially about it; but a series of demagogic charges about Adams's alleged monarchist, aristocratic, and bureaucratic prejudices served the Jackson managers for issues. Jackson got 647,000 votes, Adams 508,000.

The election of 1828 was not an uprising of the West against the East nor a triumph of the frontier: outside of New England and its colonized areas in the West, Federalist Delaware, New Jersey, and Maryland, Jackson swept the country. Nor was his election a mandate for economic reform; no financial changes, no crusades against the national bank, were promised. The main themes of Jacksonian democracy thus far were militant nationalism and equal access to office. Jackson's election was more a result than a cause of the rise of democracy, and the "revolution of 1828" more an overturn of personnel than of ideas or programs. Up to the time of his inauguration Jackson had contributed neither a thought nor a deed to the democratic movement, and he was elected without a platform. So far as he can be said to have had a popular mandate, it was to be different from what the people imagined Adams had been and to give expression to their unformulated wishes and aspirations. This mandate Jackson was prepared to obey. Democrat and aristocrat, failure and success, debtor and creditor, he had had a varied and uneven history, which made it possible for him to see public questions from more than one perspective. He was a simple, emotional, and unreflective man with a strong sense of loyalty to personal friends and political supporters; he swung to the democratic camp when the democratic camp swung to him.

III

For those who have lived through the era of Franklin D. Roosevelt it is natural to see in Jacksonian democracy an earlier version of the New Deal, for the two periods have many superficial points in common. The Jacksonian movement and the New Deal were both struggles of large sections of the community against a business elite and its allies. There is a suggestive analogy between Nicholas Biddle's political associates and the "economic royalists" of the Liberty League, and, on the other side, between the two dynamic landed aristocrats who led the popular parties. Roosevelt himself did not fail to see the resemblance and exploit it.

But the two movements differed in a critical respect: the New Deal was frankly based upon the premise that economic expansion had come to an end and economic opportunities were disappearing; it attempted to cope with the situation by establishing governmental ascendancy over the affairs of business. The Jacksonian movement grew out of expanding opportunities and a common desire to enlarge these opportunities still further by removing restrictions and privileges that had their origin in acts of government; thus, with some qualifications, it was essentially a movement of laissez-faire, an attempt to divorce government and business. It is commonly recognized in American historical folklore that the Jackson movement was a phase in the expansion of democracy, but it is too little appreciated that it was also a phase in the expansion of liberated capitalism. While in the New Deal the democratic reformers were driven to challenge many assumptions of traditional American capitalism, in the Jacksonian period the democratic upsurge was closely linked to the ambitions of the small capitalist.

To understand Jacksonian democracy it is necessary to recreate the social complexion of the United States in the 1830's. Although industrialism had begun to take root, this was still a nation of farms and small towns, which in 1830 found only one of every fifteen citizens living in cities of over 8,000. Outside the South, a sweeping majority of the people were independent property-owners. Factories had been growing in some areas, but industry was not yet concentrated in the factory system; much production was carried out in little units in which the employer was like a master craftsman supervising his apprentices. The development of transportation made it possible to extend trade over large areas, which resulted in a delay in collections and increased the dependence of business upon banks for credit facilities. The merchant capitalist found it easier to get the necessary credits than humbler masters and minor entrepreneurs, but the hope of growing more prosperous remained intensely alive in the breast of the small manufacturer and the skilled craftsman.

The flowering of manufacturing in the East, the rapid settlement of the West, gave to the spirit of enterprise a large measure of fulfillment. The typical American was an expectant capitalist, a hardworking, ambitious person for whom enterprise was a kind of religion, and everywhere he found conditions that encouraged him to extend himself. Francis J. Grund, an immigrant who described American social conditions in 1836, reported:

Business is the very soul of an American: he pursues it, not as a means of procuring for himself and his family the necessary comforts of life, but as the fountain of all human felicity. . . . It is as if all America were but one gigantic workshop, over the entrance of which there is the blazing inscription, "No admission here, except on business."

More than one type of American, caught up in this surge of ambition, had reason to be dissatisfied with the United States Bank. Some farmers were more interested in the speculative values of their lands than in their agricultural yield. Operators of wildcat banks in the South and West and speculators who depended upon wildcat loans shared the farmers' dislike of Biddle's bank for restraining credit inflation. In the East

some of the heads of strong, sound state banks were jealous of the privileged position of the national bank—particularly the bankers of New York City, who resented the financial supremacy that the bank brought to Philadelphia. In Eastern cities the bank was also widely disliked by workers, craftsmen, shopkeepers, and small business people. Labor was hard hit by the rising cost of living, and in many cases the workmen's agitation was directed not so much against their immediate employers as against the credit and currency system. Small business- and workingmen felt that banks restricted competition and prevented new men from entering upon the avenues of enterprise.

The prevalent method of granting corporation charters in the states was a source of enormous resentment. The states did not have general laws governing incorporation. Since banks and other profit-making businesses that wished to incorporate had to apply to state legislatures for individual acts of incorporation, the way was left open for favoritism and corruption. Very often the corporation charters granted by the legislatures were, or were construed to be, monopolies. Men whose capital or influence was too small to gain charters from the lawmakers were barred from such profitable and strategic lines of corporate enterprise as banks, bridges, railroads, turnpikes, and ferries. The practice was looked upon as an artificial closure of opportunity: laborers often blamed it for the high price of necessities. The practice of granting economic privileges was also considered a threat to popular government. Jackson, explaining in one of his presidential messages why "the planter, the farmer, the mechanic, and the laborer" were "in constant danger of losing their fair interest in the Government," had a standard answer: "The mischief springs from the power which the moneyed interest derives from a paper currency, which they are able to control, from the multitude of corporations with exclusive privileges which they have succeeded in obtaining in the different States."

Among all the exclusive privileged monopolies in the country the Bank of the United States was the largest, the best-known, and the most powerful. It became a symbol for all the others, and the burden of many grievances for which it was not really responsible fell upon it. As a national institution it was doubly vulnerable: it was blamed by Western inflationists for deflationary policies and by Eastern hard-money men for inflation. One certain accomplishment of Jackson's war on the bank was to discharge the aggressions of citizens who felt injured by economic privilege.

Jackson himself was by no means unfamiliar with the entrepreneurial impulse that gave Jacksonian democracy so much of its freshness and vitality. An enterpriser of middling success, he could spontaneously see things from the standpoint of the typical American who was eager for advancement in the democratic game of competition—the master mechanic who aspired to open his own shop, the planter or farmer who speculated in land, the lawyer who hoped to be a judge, the local politician who wanted to go to Congress, the grocer who would be a merchant. He had entered the scramble himself in a variety of lines, as a professional man, a merchant, a land speculator, a planter, an officeholder, and a military chieftain. He understood the old Jeffersonian's bias against overgrown government machinery, the Westerner's resentment of the entrenched East, the new politician's dislike of the old bureaucracy, and the aspiring citizen's hatred of privilege. Years before his presidency, he recalled, when a few Tennesseans proposed in 1817 to bring a branch of the bank to Nashville, he had opposed it on the ground that the bank "would drain the state of its specie to the amount of its profits for the support and prosperity of other places, and the Lords, Dukes, and Ladies of foreign countries who held the greater part of its stock—no individual but one in our state owning any of its stock." In 1827, when a branch of the bank was finally created at Nashville, and its agent, General Thomas Cadwalader, coyly hinted to Jackson that its patronage could be turned over to the Jackson party, he was rebuffed.

Looking at the bank from the White House, Jackson saw an instrument of great privilege and power ruled by a man of uncommon force and intelligence. As a fiscal agency it was comparable in magnitude to the government itself. It issued about one fourth of the country's bank paper; because of its power over the discounts of innumerable smaller banks, especially in the West and South, it was the only central instrument in the United States that could affect the volume of credit. A private agency performing a major public function, it was yet substantially free of government control. As Hezekiah Niles put it, the bank had "more power than we would grant to any set of men unless responsible to the people." Nicholas Biddle, boasting of the forbearance with which he ran the bank, once stated in a Congressional investigation that there were "very few banks which might not have been destroyed by an exertion of the powers of the Bank." "As to mere power," he wrote to Thomas Cooper in 1837, "I have been for years in the daily exercise of more personal authority than any President habitually enjoys." Understandably the bank's critics regarded it as a potential menace to democratic institutions.

As an economic instrument, there was a great deal to be said for the bank. Under Biddle it had done a creditable job in stabilizing the currency and holding in check inflationary pressure from the wildcatters. Before Jackson's election Biddle had also been concerned to keep the bank out of partisan politics and, as he wrote Webster, "bring it down to its true business character as a Counting House." But the bank inspired too many animosities to stay out of political life. After 1829 it had large loans outstanding to a great number of prominent politicians and influential newspaper editors, and Biddle was well aware how great its power would be if it should be employed directly in corruption. "I can remove all the constitutional scruples in the District of Columbia," he arrogantly informed a correspondent in 1833. "Half a dozen Presidencies—a dozen Cashierships—fifty Clerkships—a hundred Directorships—to worthy friends who have no character and no money."

Since the bank's charter was to expire in 1836, and since a second term for Jackson was probable, it seemed necessary that a renewal of the charter be secured under Jackson. Biddle attempted at first to be conciliatory, made earnest efforts to answer Jackson's grievances against the bank, appointed Jacksonian politicians to several branch directorships, and sent the President a not ungenerous proposal for assistance in discharging the government's indebtedness in return for recharter. Yet in the fall or winter of 1829–30, when Biddle and Jackson had an amicable interview, the general frankly said: "I do not dislike your Bank any more than all banks. But ever since I read the history of the South Sea bubble I have been afraid of banks."

By December 1830, when Jackson questioned the bank's expediency and constitutionality, it was clear that he would not consent to renew its life. Biddle, reluctantly, uncertainly, and under prodding from Whig politicians, decided in the summer of 1832 to ask Congress for recharter before the presidential election. "The bank," said Jackson to Van Buren, "is trying to kill me, *but I will kill it!*" To the frontier duelist the issue had instantly become personal.

Jackson lost no time in returning the recharter bill to Congress with his famous veto message, described by Biddle as "a manifesto of anarchy, such as Marat and Robespierre might have issued to the mob." The body of the message was an argument against the bank's constitutionality. The social indictment of the bank was inclusive: it was a monopoly, a grant of exclusive privilege; the whole American people were excluded from competition in the sale of the privilege, and the government thus received less than it was worth; a fourth of the bank's stock was held by foreigners, the rest by "a few hundred of our citizens, chiefly of the richest class"; it was a menace to the country's liberty and independence. At the end the President launched into a forthright statement of the social philosophy of the Jacksonian movement:

It is to be regretted that the rich and powerful too often bend the acts of government to their selfish purposes. Distinctions in society will always exist under every just government. Equality of talents, of education, or of wealth cannot be produced by human institutions. In the full enjoyment of the gifts of Heaven and the fruits of superior industry, economy, and virtue, every man is equally entitled to protection by law; but when the laws undertake to add to these natural and just advantages artificial distinctions, to grant titles, gratuities, and exclusive privileges, to make the rich richer and the potent more powerful, the humble members of society—the farmers, mechanics, and laborers—who have neither the time nor the means of securing like favors to themselves, have a right to complain of the injustice of their Government. There are no necessary evils in government. Its evils exist only in its abuses. If it would confine itself to equal protection, and, as Heaven does its rains, shower its favors alike on the high and the low, the rich and the poor, it would be an unqualified blessing.

Certainly this is not the philosophy of a radical leveling movement that proposes to uproot property or to reconstruct society along drastically different lines. It proceeds upon no Utopian premises—full equality is impossible, "distinctions will always exist," and reward should rightly go to "superior industry, economy, and virtue." What is demanded is only the classic bourgeois ideal, equality before the law, the restriction of government to equal protection of its citizens. This is the philosophy of a rising middle class; its aim is not to throttle but to liberate business, to open every possible pathway for the creative enterprise of the people. Although the Jacksonian leaders were more aggressive than the Jeffersonians in their crusades against monopoly and "the paper system," it is evident that the core of their philosophy was the same: both aimed to take the grip of government-granted privileges off the natural economic order. It was no coincidence that Jacksonians like William Leggett and Thomas Hart Benton still venerated John Taylor, a thinker of what Jackson affectionately called "the old republican school."

IV

Pursuing the bank war to its conclusion, Jackson found defeat in victory. Re-elected overwhelmingly on the bank issue in 1832, he soon removed all United States funds from the bank. Biddle, in the course of a fight to get the federal deposits back, brought about a short-lived but severe depression through restriction of credit, which ended only when the business community itself rebelled. No sooner did this artificial depression end than an inflationary movement began. The federal deposits that Jackson had taken from Biddle were made available to several dozen state banks; these promptly used their new resources to start a credit boom, which broke disastrously in 1837. This had been no part of Jackson's original intention, nor that of his hard-money followers. "I did not join in putting down the Bank of the United States," complained Thomas Hart Benton, "to put up a wilderness of local banks." By destroying Biddle's bank Jackson had taken away the only effective restraint on the wildcatters, and by distributing the deposits had enlarged the capital in the hands of inflationists. He was opposed to both privilege and inflation, but in warring on one he had succeeded only in releasing the other. In killing the bank he had strangled a potential threat to democratic government, but at an unnecessarily high cost. He had caused Biddle to create one depression and the pet banks to aggravate a second, and he had left the nation committed to a currency and credit system even more inadequate than the one he had inherited.

Biddle, from 1823, when he took control of the bank, to 1833, when removal of the deposits provoked him to outrageous retaliation, had followed a policy of gradual, controlled credit expansion, which was well adapted to the needs of the growing American economy. Had Jackson not yielded to archaic hard-money theories on one hand and the pressure of interested inflationary groups on the other, it might have been possible—and it would have been far wiser—

for him to have made a deal with Biddle, trading recharter of the bank for more adequate government control of the bank's affairs. It would have been possible to safeguard democratic institutions without such financial havoc, but the Jacksonians were caught between their hostility to the bank and their unwillingness to supplant it with adequate federal control of credit. The popular hatred of privilege and the dominant laissez-faire ideology made an unhappy combination.

The bank war flared up, died, and was forgotten, its permanent results negative rather than positive. But the struggle against corporate privileges which it symbolized was waged on a much wider front. In the states this struggle bore fruit in a series of general incorporation acts, beginning with Connecticut's in 1837 and spreading to the other states in the two decades before the Civil War. By opening the process of incorporation to all comers who could meet state requirements, legislators progressively sundered the concept of the corporate form of business from its association with monopoly privilege and for many decades made it an element in the growth of free enterprise—a contribution to the development of American business that can hardly be overestimated. The same was done for banking. In 1838 New York, the center of the Locofoco agitation against bank monopolies, passed a free banking law that permitted banking associations to operate under general rules without applying for specific acts of incorporation. A precedent for similar laws in other states, it has been described by one authority, Bray Hammond, as "the most important event in American banking history."

While the state legislatures were writing Jacksonian ideals into the law of corporations, a Jacksonian Supreme Court under Chief Justice Taney was reading them into the clauses of the Constitution. Taney, appointed by Jackson in 1836, sat on the Court until his death in 1864, and during his long tenure the Court propagated the Jacksonian view of business without privilege. Professor Benjamin F. Wright, in his study of *The Contract Clause of the Constitution,* has pointed out that as a result of the Court's work under Taney the contract clause "was a more secure and broader base for the defense of property rights in 1864 than it had been in 1835." Taney's most startling case, as symbolic of the fight against privilege in the juridical sphere as the bank war had been in politics, was the Charles River Bridge case. The majority decision, prepared by Taney, which represented a long forward step in detaching from the corporation the stigma of monopoly, stands as a classic statement of the Jacksonian faith.

The Charles River Bridge had been erected in the 1780's by Harvard College and prominent Bostonians under a Massachusetts charter. As the population of Boston and Cambridge grew, business flourished, traffic mounted, and the par value of the bridge's stock shot upwards. A share bought in 1805 at $444 was worth $2,080 in 1814. Since a new bridge was badly needed, the state legislature in 1828 chartered another, the Warren Bridge, to be built very close to the original, and to be free after sufficient tolls were collected to pay for its construction. Anxious to prevent a development that would destroy the value of their stock, the proprietors of the older bridge attempted to restrain the new builders from erecting the Warren Bridge. When Taney began sitting as Chief Justice in 1837, the issue was still pending before the Supreme Court. The case clearly involved a conflict between vested rights on one side and new entrepreneurs and the rest of the community on the other. Four distinguished Massachusetts lawyers, including Daniel Webster, represented the promoters of the Charles River Bridge. They argued that the legislative grant to the original bridge company was a contract, and that implicit in such a ferry or bridge franchise was a promise on the part of the state not to break the contract by granting another competing franchise that would lower the value of the original.

The Court decided for the new bridge, five to two. Since the two dissenting justices, Story and Thompson, were holdovers from the pre-Jackson period and the five majority judges were all Jackson appointees, the decision may accurately be called a Jacksonian document. Story's dissent, which expressed horror at "speculative niceties or novelties" and invoked the interests of "every stockholder in every public enterprise of this sort throughout the country," was reasoned in the language of entrenched capital, of monopoly investors who abhorred risk. Taney's majority decision was a plea for the public interest, for technological progress and fresh enterprise.

The object of all government, Taney asserted, is to promote the happiness and prosperity of the community, and it could never be assumed that a government intended to curtail its own powers in this respect. "And in a country like ours, free, active, and enterprising, continually advancing in numbers and wealth," new channels of communication and travel are continually found necessary; an abandonment of the state's power to facilitate new developments should not be construed from contracts that do not contain an explicit statement of such intent.

What would happen, Taney asked, if the idea of an implied monopoly in charters should be sustained by the Court? What would become of the numerous railroads established on the same line of travel with old turnpike companies? He thought he knew: if these old corporations were given an "undefined property in a line of travelling," they would awaken from their sleep and call upon the Court to put down new improvements to protect their vested interests. The "millions of property" that had been invested in railroads and canals upon lines of travel once occupied by turnpike corporations would be endangered. Until obsolete claims were settled, the community would be deprived of the benefits of invention enjoyed by every other part of the civilized world. The rights of property, Taney conceded, should be "sacredly guarded," but "we must not forget that the community also have rights, and that the happiness and well-being of every citizen depends upon their faithful preservation."

To the Whig press and conservative lawyers like Kent and Story this opinion appeared as another "manifesto of anarchy," comparable to Jackson's bank veto message. In fact, as Charles Warren observes in his history of the Court, it gave encouragement to "all business men who contemplated investments of capital in new corporate enterprise and who were relieved against claims of monopoly concealed in ambiguous clauses of old charters."

In the Congressional session of 1823–4, at the beginning of the Jackson era, Daniel Webster had observed: "Society is full of excitement: competition comes in place of monopoly; and intelligence and industry ask only for fair play and an open field." No friend of Jacksonian democracy expressed more accurately than this opponent the historic significance of the Jackson movement. With Old Hickory's election a fluid economic and social system broke the bonds of a fixed and stratified political order. Originally a fight against political privilege, the Jacksonian movement had broadened into a fight against economic privilege, rallying to its support a host of "rural capitalists and village entrepreneurs." When Jackson left office he was the hero of the lower and middling elements of American society who believed in expanding opportunity through equal rights, and by the time of his death in 1845 the "excitement" Webster had noticed had left a deep and lasting mark upon the nation. "This," exulted Calvin Colton, "is a country of self-made men, than which there can be no better in any state of society."

Bray Hammond: THE JACKSONIANS

Bray Hammond, a former secretary of the Federal Reserve Board, has become the foremost historian in our time of the history of banking in the United States in the early decades of the nineteenth Century. His full-scale study of Banks and Politics in America *from the Revolution to the Civil War (1957) displays a particular animus toward the argument that the Jacksonian attack on the United States Bank was thought out and carried out by agrarian reformers and labor groups. In Hammond's interpretation, Jackson can be conceived of as "the champion of the common man" only if we recognize that this was a new kind of common man. "This new common man was manufacturer, banker, builder, carrier, and promoter." The following selection illustrates the way in which Hammond identifies the economic backgrounds and the motives of the Jacksonians.*

I

DURING the half century that ended with General Jackson's election, America underwent changes perhaps the most radical and sweeping it has ever undergone in so short a time. It passed the climacteric separating a modern industrial economy from an older one of handicraft; it passed from colonial weakness through bare independence to actual power and from an unjostled rural culture to the complexities of populousness, sectionalism, urban slums, mechanized industry, and monetary credit. Men who had spent their childhood in a thin line of seaboard colonies, close even in their little cities to the edge of the westward continental wilderness, spent their late years in a tamed and wealthy land spread already to the Missouri and about to extend beyond it. They lived to ride on railways and steamships, to use the products of steam-driven machinery, to dwell in metropolitan centers, and to feel within their grasp and the grasp of their sons more potential and accessible wealth than had ever before excited the enterprise of man.

An outstanding factor in the changes that came about was the flow of immigration from Europe. Between 1790 and 1840 the population grew from 4,000,000 to 17,000,000. In the latter year an average of 230 immigrants entered the country daily. Ten years later it was over 1,000 daily. The area of settlement and exploitation expanded swiftly under the pressure of this movement. While General Jackson was President the federal union came to include twice as many states as it had begun with and held territory that recently had belonged to Spain and France. It was shortly to add regions in the South and West taken from Mexico and regions in the Northwest that Great Britain claimed. Its expansion seemed irresistible.

The changes in social outlook were profound. Steam was generating conceptions of life, liberty, and the pursuit of happiness that were quite alien to Thomas Jefferson's; and the newcomers pushing into the country from Europe had more impatient economic motives than their 18th century predecessors. People were led as they had not been before by visions of money-making. Liberty became transformed into *laisser faire*. A violent, aggressive, economic individualism became established. The democracy became greedy, intolerant, imperialistic, and lawless. It opened economic advantages to those who had not previously had them; yet it allowed wealth to be concentrated in new hands

only somewhat more numerous than before, less responsible, and less disciplined. There were unenterprising and unpropertied thousands who missed entirely the economic opportunities with which America was thick. There was poverty in the eastern cities and poverty on the frontier. Those who failed to hold their own in the struggle were set down as unfit.

Wealth was won and lost, lost and won. Patient accumulation was contemned. People believed it was not what they saved but what they made that counted. Jay Cooke, one of America's future millionaires, who was scarcely born poor on a farm but primitively at least, in a frontier settlement, was already on his way to fortune in a private banking firm before the age of twenty and writing home about his work with enthusiasm. This was in the winter of 1839–1840. "My bosses are making money fast," he said. "This business is always good, and those who follow it in time become rich. . . . Among our customers are men of every age and every position in society, from the hoary miser to the dashing buck who lives upon his thousands. Through all grades I see the same all-pervading, all-engrossing anxiety to grow rich." Something of the same sort, to be sure, was taking place in Western Europe and especially in Great Britain. Half the people and most of the money for America's transformation came from there. But though industrial and technological revolution occurred also in the Old World, in the New, where vast resources awaited exploitation, it produced a dazzling, democratic expansion experienced nowhere else. The situation was such that the rallying cry, *"Laissez nous faire!"* expressed the views of Americans perfectly, when translated.

Socially, the Jacksonian revolution signified that a nation of democrats was tired of being governed, however well, by gentlemen from Virginia and Massachusetts. As Professor Sumner observed, what seems to have enchanted people with General Jackson when he became a candidate for President was not any principles or policies he advocated but his breaches of decorum, real or alleged. Economically, the revolution signified that a nation of potential money-makers could not abide traditionary, conservative limitations on business enterprise, particularly by capitalists in Philadelphia. The Jacksonian revolution was a consequence of the Industrial Revolution and of a farm-born people's realization that now anyone in America could get rich and through his own efforts, if he had a fair chance. A conception of earned wealth arose which rendered the self-made man as superior morally to the hereditary well-to-do as the agrarian had been. It was like the conception which led Theodoric the Great to boast that he held Italy solely by right of conquest and without the shadow of legal, that is, hereditary right. The humbly born and rugged individualists who were gaining fortunes by their own toil and sweat, or wits, were still simple Americans, Jeffersonian, anti-monopolistic, anti-governmental, but fraught with the spirit of enterprise and fired with a sense of what soon would be called manifest destiny. They envied the social and economic advantages of the established urban capitalists, mercantile and financial; and they fought these aristocrats with far more zeal and ingenuity than the agrarians ever had. They resented the federal Bank's interference with expansion of the monetary supply. They found it bestriding the path of enterprise, and with Apollyon's brag but Christian's better luck they were resolved to spill its soul.

They democratized business under a great show of agrarian idealism and made the age of Jackson a festival of *laisser faire* prelusive to the age of Grant and the robber barons.

In their attack on the Bank of the United States, the Jacksonians still employed the vocabulary of their agrarian backgrounds. The phraseology of idealism was adapted to money-making, the creed of an earlier generation becoming the cant of its successor. Their terms of abuse were "oppression," "tyranny," "monied power," "aristocracy," "wealth," "privilege," "monopoly"; their terms of praise were "the humble," "the poor," "the simple," "the honest and industrious." Though their cause was a sophisticated one of enterpriser against capitalist, of banker against regulation, and of Wall Street against Chestnut, the language was the same as if they were all back on the farm. Neither the President, nor his advisers, nor their followers saw any discrepancy between the concept of freedom in an age of agrarianism and the concept of freedom in one of enterprise. Only the poets and philosophers were really aware that a discrepancy existed and though troubled by it their vision was far from clear. Notwithstanding their language, therefore, the Jacksonians' destruction of the Bank of the United States was in no sense a blow at capitalism or property or the "money power." It was a blow at an older set of capitalists by a newer, more numerous set. It was incident to the democratization of business, the diffusion of enterprise among the mass of people, and the transfer of economic primacy from an old and conservative merchant class to a newer, more aggressive, and more numerous body of businessmen and speculators of all sorts.

The Jacksonians were unconventional

and skillful in politics. In their assault on the Bank they united five important elements, which, incongruities notwithstanding, comprised an effective combination. These were Wall Street's jealousy of Chestnut Street, the business man's dislike of the federal Bank's restraint upon bank credit, the politician's resentment at the Bank's interference with states' rights, popular identification of the Bank with the aristocracy of business, and the direction of agrarian antipathy away from banks in general to the federal Bank in particular. Destruction of the Bank ended federal regulation of bank credit and shifted the money center of the country from Chestnut Street to Wall Street. It left the poor agrarian as poor as he had been before and it left the money power possessed of more money and more power than ever.

II

By the term "Jacksonian" I mean not merely the President's Democratic supporters, whom he still called Republican, but in particular his closest advisers and sharers in responsibility. These included most of his "Kitchen Cabinet," some of his official Cabinet, and a number of others. Those most responsible for the destruction of the Bank, without whose urgency and help it might not have been undertaken or achieved, were all either businessmen or closely concerned with the business world. Named in the approximate order of their appearance, they were Duff Green, Samuel Ingham, Isaac Hill, Martin Van Buren, Amos Kendall, Francis Preston Blair, Churchill C. Cambreleng, Roger B. Taney, and David Henshaw—all but Taney being or becoming men of wealth. They did not include Major William B. Lewis, a Tennessee planter, one of the General's oldest friends and the only one of his intimates not openly hostile to the Bank. Others of importance were Thomas Hart Benton, James K. Polk, Levi Woodbury, Benjamin F. Butler, Jacob Barker, Reuben M. Whitney, William Gouge, and James A. Hamilton.

Duff Green was born in Kentucky but as a young man he went on to Missouri, where he became a land speculator and merchant, with a substantial business centering in St. Louis. By the time he left there a decade later, he says: "I had established the first line of stages west of the Mississippi. I had a profitable contract for carrying the mail. I had placed the line under the charge of trustworthy partners, who paid me a large fixed income. I had a valuable business as an attorney. I was the editor and proprietor of a leading paper, giving me considerable profit, and I was investing my income in and adjoining the city of St. Louis." He moved to Washington in 1825, where he owned the *United States Telegraph* and edited it in support of Andrew Jackson for President and in denunciation of the Bank of the United States. Newspaper publishing was apparently a simpler, less specialized, and perhaps more generally profitable form of business then than it has since become. He at first belonged to the Kitchen Cabinet, but before long he was thrust out because he was a friend of John C. Calhoun. Though Duff Green borrowed from the Bank, he approved its destruction. But his dislike of it was offset by his dislike of Amos Kendall and other Jacksonians and by his ties of family and friendship with Mr. Calhoun. He continued a long, successful career in business enterprise, being banker, railway-builder, manufacturer, and promoter in divers fields.

Andrew Jackson's first Secretary of the Treasury was Samuel Ingham of

Pennsylvania, farm-born but apprenticed to a paper-maker. He remained active in farming while engaged mainly in paper-manufacturing, coal-mining, railways, and eventually banking. Though primarily a business man he was always active in politics. As Secretary of the Treasury he opened the official assault on the federal Bank.

An assistant of his in the Treasury who instigated the attack was Isaac Hill of New Hampshire, also an appointee of General Jackson's. He was frail and lame, an abusive editorial-writer, an acrid partisan, a publisher, a bank director, a bank president, and a substantial man of business. He too was a member of the Kitchen Cabinet. He failed to be confirmed in his Treasury appointment by the Senate, but promptly got elected a member thereof. As an editor, in Professor Sumner's words, "His main 'principle' was that things were in the hands of an 'aristocracy' and that he ought to organize the 'honest yeomanry' in order to oust that aristocracy from power. . . . He had the rancorous malignity of those men who have been in a contest with persons who have treated them from above downwards." When a candidate for Governor of New Hampshire in 1835 he had to be defended from the "grave reproach" of being wealthy. But if wealthy, it was urged, he had not always been so; "Isaac Hill was born of poor but respectable parentage." He was a self-made man and not one of "those sons of fortune who have been from their very cradle nursed in the lap of luxury, who have never known what it is to grapple with adversity, who have found every wish anticipated and every want supplied almost before it was experienced." Such "may thank their God that they are not as this mechanic," but they "will generally be found, in their race through

life, . . . outstripped by those whose experience and whose training have prepared them by their very severity for a certain victory."

Martin Van Buren, President Jackson's first Secretary of State, later Vice President with him, and his successor in the Presidency, was probably the most influential of the President's advisers and highest in his esteem. His father had been a farmer and tavern-keeper of very modest estate, and he himself was without formal education. He achieved polish, eminence, and wealth. In his early career he was an associate of Jacob Barker, a Wall Street banker of more enterprise than substance. He left the bar at the age of forty-six, when he became Governor of New York, "with a competence fairly earned, which his prudence and skill made grow into an ample fortune." Baring Brothers were informed by a New York correspondent, the banker Jonathan Goodhue, 16 March 1837, respecting the new President, that "Mr. Van Buren is a very rich man," with an understanding of business "vastly better" than General Jackson's. The Albany Regency, the New York political oligarchy of which he was the creative spirit, maintained banks and politics in the most intimate union. Mr. Van Buren sponsored, as Governor, a law enacted in 1829 authorizing a system of state banks under a Safety Fund. He was always an efficient promoter of New York's economic interests. He did not openly oppose the Bank of the United States till late, or even then conspicuously, and Nicholas Biddle long refused to believe he was not the friend he had seemed to be. Mr. Van Buren's tact was extraordinary; he had superlative skill in political manipulation and the advancement of his own interest without friction or apparent effort. Though self-made, like most of the men on whom General Jackson relied, Mr. Van Buren differed from the others in performing his task with modesty and grace; he was without rancor, without assertiveness, and without the psychotic sense of insecurity and inferiority that seemed to torment many of his Jacksonian associates.

Francis Preston Blair replaced Duff Green as journalist spokesman of the Jacksonians. The new journal set up for him was the *Globe*. Amos Kendall said the *Globe* was originated by "those friends of General Jackson who regarded measures more than men and desired his re-election for another four years, not so much for his own sake, as to effect reforms in the government which no other man was capable of bringing about." Chief of these reforms, Mr. Kendall said, was an end to the Bank. Blair, the *Globe's* proprietor, had been president of the Commonwealth Bank of Kentucky and co-editor with Amos Kendall of the *Argus of Western America*. He was "heavily indebted" to the Bank of the United States—the amount exceeded $20,000—but the difficulty was got around by a settlement at about ten cents on the dollar, and he was fetched to Washington, where he began publication of the *Globe* in December 1830. The paper was very profitable and with the government printing made Blair a rich man.

Amos Kendall was a native of New England, the son of a typically poor but independent Massachusetts farmer of a typically puritan background. He was educated at Dartmouth. In 1814 he emigrated to Kentucky, where in time he became proprietor and editor in Frankfort of the *Argus of Western America*. Although scarcely a personal acquaintance before they came to Washington, Mr. Kendall became invaluable to President Jackson directly thereafter. He was

foremost in the Kitchen Cabinet. He held the office of Fourth Auditor of the Treasury but was far beyond his official superiors in influence. It was said that "whatever Kendall went for he fetched." He was known to the generality in Washington as an invincible, sallow, white-haired, unhealthy creature, but seldom seen. Harriet Martineau was fortunate enough to catch a glimpse of him once, and a Congressman who saw him at the same time told her that "he had watched through four sessions for a sight of Kendall and had never obtained it till now." The "invisible Amos Kendall," she reported, was "one of the most remarkable men in America, . . . supposed to be the moving spring of the whole administration; the thinker, planner, and doer; but it is all in the dark." His were the terse and commanding words repeated daily in the Jacksonian press: "The world is governed too much." Being made Postmaster General in 1835, he showed signal administrative ability in reforming the postal service. In 1845 he became associated with Samuel F. B. Morse in the commercial development of the telegraph. He had found Mr. Morse "endeavoring, with little prospect of success, to get an appropriation from Congress to extend a line of his telegraph from Baltimore to New York; it being already in operation between Washington and Baltimore." He asked Mr. Morse "whether he had no project to render his telegraph profitable as a private enterprise." Out of his enquiry an agreement arose which "vested Mr. Kendall with full power to manage and dispose of Morse's interest in his patent-right, according to his discretion." And from this in turn came the erection of telegraph lines everywhere in the country, determined suits in defense of patents, the formation of numerous separate companies, and their eventual consolidation into a nation-wide system. One could not imagine a more explicit example of entrepreneurial behavior. Mr. Kendall fought his way to such wealth and success that in time he had to defend himself from the charge, echoing one he had so often made against the Bank of the United States, that he and his business associates were "autocrats of the telegraph" and that "a more infamous monopoly than the American Telegraph Company" never existed. With Mr. Van Buren, whose talents were of a different order, he was the ablest of the Jacksonians and an outstanding figure in American business enterprise.

Mr. Kendall's progress was a consistent one. As early as 1820 he was denying that labor was a source of value. He had always taken a harsh, puritanical view of things and scorned governmental relief in the days of western distress. He had favored "some degree of relief" but condemned Kentucky's interference with foreclosures. "Things will take their course in the moral as well as in the natural world," he had written. Legislatures could not relieve man of his responsibilities. "The people must pay their own debts at last." He had considered the Bank of the United States an artificial monopoly poisonous to individualism and its annihilation the paramount aim of "the Democracy." Speaking years later of "reforms in the government" in which he had participated, he said that "chief of these was its severance from the banking power organized and exercised under the charter of the Bank of the United States." It was his belief that Congress should "be content to let currency and private business alone." He never abandoned this view. He was an apostle and exemplar of *laisser faire*. Government,

he said, "cannot make the people rich but may make them poor." Americans, in his opinion, were demanding "that their governments shall content themselves with protecting their persons and property, leaving them to direct their labor and capital as they please, within the moral law; getting rich or remaining poor as may result from their own management or fortune." Mr. Kendall turned to religion and philanthropy in his later years; he was a founder and benefactor of what is now Gallaudet College, for the deaf, Kendall Green, Washington, D.C. It was the only such college in the world, and he was its first president.

Churchill C. Cambreleng, member of Congress from New York City, was a close associate of Martin Van Buren and an administration leader in the lower house, where he was known as New York's "commercial representative." He was a self-made man of modest North Carolina origins who had become a confidential agent and friend of John Jacob Astor. He had been friendly to the Bank of the United States before Jackson's election. About 1825 he had visited western New York at the request of the Bank, and for a fee, to study the relative advantages of Rochester, Utica, and Buffalo for a new branch office to be established in that region. He understood the operations of the Bank fully; Nicholas Biddle said it would be "difficult to describe more accurately the plan of circulation of the Bank" than he had done. Like Martin Van Buren, Mr. Cambreleng was an efficient promoter of New York's interests, both political and economic. He was tireless and highly capable in his congressional leadership against the Bank.

Roger B. Taney (pronounced Tawney) was President Jackson's second Attorney General and his fourth Treasury Secretary. He shared first place with Kendall and Cambreleng among the President's advisers in relentless, aggressive, resourceful enmity for the Bank of the United States. He was a Baltimore attorney and member of a family belonging to the landed aristocracy of southern Maryland, where he was reared. He was a shareholder in the Union Bank of Baltimore, its counsel, and an intimate friend of its president, Thomas Ellicott. This bank was one to which federal funds were transferred when he and President Jackson removed them from the federal Bank. Mr. Taney had been interested previously in three other banks and a director of two. In an influential letter to President Jackson, 27 June 1832, he denied the constitutionality and expediency of the Bank on the ground that it bestowed privileges on some and refused them to others. He ignored the regulatory duties of the government and of the Bank, except as an "absolute dominance over the circulating medium of the country," and confined the Bank's usefulness to its safekeeping and transport of federal funds. As he disingenuously put it, "the simple question of selecting the most appropriate agent for conveying the public revenues from place to place has excited as much heat and passion as even the great question of the tariff." The question was not the simple one he said it was, and the regulation of banking and money is no less important than the tariff. He dwelt on the unfairness to the state banks of chartering a federal Bank, exempt from state taxation, on "the burthens now borne by the state banks," and on the "heavy impositions" invidiously put on "the property of individuals in the state banks." For, he said, "the stockholders in the state banks, who

are generally men in moderate circumstances, are subject to the weight of unlimited war taxation whenever the public exigency may require it—why should the stock in the Bank of the United States, which is generally held by the most opulent monied men, many of them wealthy foreigners, be entirely free from the additional taxation which war or any other calamity may bring upon the rest of the community? . . . The money of the citizens employed in the state banks is to be diminished in value by new burthens whenever the wants of the country require it, while the money of the opulent citizen and of the wealthy foreigner . . . is not to be allowed to feel the pressure. . . ." This was false. No such line could be drawn between the wealth of the federal Bank's stockholders and that of state bank stockholders, nor had the federal Bank any immunity from taxation, save by the states.

Mr. Taney was eventually appointed Chief Justice of the Supreme Court by President Jackson, where his decisions regularly favored free enterprise and competition—and typically so in the Charles River Bridge case, 1837. In this major decision he denied that rights had been vested in one toll-bridge corporation which must be allowed to obstruct the erection of other bridges needed by the community. The rights of the first, the Charles River Bridge, ran back by succession almost two centuries to a legislative grant to Harvard College for a ferry between Cambridge and Boston. The income from tolls on the bridge that replaced the ferry made it a very profitable investment. But one bridge in time proved not to be enough: and the new bridge that was built being eventually passable without toll, to the loss of income and investment by the Charles

River Bridge's proprietors, the latter sued in the Supreme Court for redress. Their suit was rejected. The State, according to Taney's opinion, could not be supposed to have surrendered "its power of improvement and public accommodation in a great and important line of travel along which a vast number of its citizens must daily pass." For though the rights of property are to be "sacredly guarded, we must not forget that the community also have rights and that the happiness and well-being of every citizen depends on their faithful preservation." Especially "in a country like ours," declared Chief Justice Taney, "free, active, and enterprising, continually advancing in numbers and wealth, new channels of communication are daily found necessary, both for travel and trade, and are essential to the comfort, convenience, and prosperity of the people."

It does not derogate from the propriety of this opinion to point out that though it is compatible with agrarian doctrine its real affinity is with *laisser faire*. It favored free enterprise, and at the same time it contributed to a new concept of the corporation. Though it seemed at the moment a blow at corporate rights in the sense that it refused to preserve a monopoly of bridge traffic anciently conferred, its beneficiary was not an individual or several individuals but a new and rival corporation competing with the old. It therefore further familiarized people with corporate competition as well as corporate monopoly and definitely helped the corporation replace the individual as an agent of free enterprise in the economy. Mr. Taney, I am sure, intended no such eventuality. Nor, I am sure, did Justice Story and Daniel Webster, by insisting on the preservation of the rights long vested in the original bridge company, intend that future material progress be shackled to 17th century grants appropriate to 17th century life. But Taney just as surely was on the side of *laisser faire* and rampant business individualism as Story and Webster were on the side of economic and technical conservatism. He was not attacking vested rights *per se*, or corporate rights, or property rights, or wealth, or capitalism, but propounding a new democratic concept that within his own lifetime was to be more typical of capitalism than was the clumsy, antediluvian monopoly that he refused to sanction.

And so of his interposition in banking —to say that it was agrarian and anticapitalistic is absurd. By siding with the state banks against the federal Bank, he simply contributed to a new and democratic concept then current, which in New York in 1838 achieved what at the time seemed one of the notable glories of the age of Jackson—the authorization of "free banking." Yet even if *laisser faire* be deemed beneficent on the whole, it does not follow that it was properly applicable to the monetary function or warranted Taney's advocacy, in Horace Binney's words, of "an unregulated, uncontrolled, state bank paper currency." The monetary function is within the province of governmental responsibility, and though Mr. Taney and the other Jacksonians did not deny it, they did deny, to their own stultification, that banking was a monetary function. Instead they were interested in banking for the good, earthy reason that it was a fine way to make money. As Secretary of the Treasury in the Cabinet of a President who believed banks to be unconstitutional as well as morally evil, Mr. Taney said publicly and officially that "there is perhaps no business which yields a profit so certain and liberal as the business of banking and exchange; and it is proper that it should be open as far as practicable to the most free competition and its advantages shared by all classes of society." Mr. Taney made little money himself but both in administrative office and on the bench he propounded the philosophy of competitive enterprise with remarkable success. And such was his command of the arts of sycophancy and misrepresentation—always, however, in furtherance of democratic rights—that he readily got the old hero he served to face the opposite way from his real convictions and knife his own agrarian cause.

David Henshaw, one of the most important business men who helped in the assault on the federal Bank, was a poor farmer boy who became a banker, a railway-builder, newspaper-publisher, business-promoter generally, Collector of the Port of Boston, and Jacksonian political boss of Massachusetts. "Though a wealthy man," Professor Arthur M. Schlesinger, Jr., observes, "Henshaw had many of the prejudices of his humble origin. His personal rancor toward the aristocracy which had snubbed him was not unlike that of his good friend, Isaac Hill." Professor Arthur B. Darling says of Henshaw and his associates that "in order to develop political influence over the poorer classes, they themselves made capital of their hostility toward the wealthy." Henshaw's *Remarks upon the Bank of the United States*, 1831, and his proposal in 1832 for a new bank with $50,000,000 of Jacksonian capital which should replace the aristocratic monster in Philadelphia that had a capital of only $35,000,000, were echoed in the message President Jackson sent to Congress when he vetoed the federal Bank's charter in 1832. His arguments were echoed again in the reasons given to Congress by Secretary Taney in 1833 for having ceased to deposit the public funds in the public Bank. "Even if it be expedient to grant a Bank upon the same plan," Henshaw said, "it ought not to be exclusively to the present stockholders. . . . The whole community should be offered the opportunity to have an interest in the institution on equal terms." This argument, though false in its implication, impressed the President. Henshaw in 1830 had deposited in his own bank the public funds he took in as Collector of the Port of Boston, thus pioneering in the action that Jackson and Taney took three years later in removing the federal funds from the federal depository and putting them in pet state banks.

David Henshaw's views on vested rights received still more formidable confirmation. Having had land to sell in South Boston to which free access must be provided, he and his associates had built a bridge, given it to the state, and sold the land profitably. Later Henshaw championed the new Warren Bridge against the old Charles River Bridge in the controversy to which I have just referred in speaking of Roger B. Taney. He was scorned by the more intellectual and idealistic Jacksonians, but the irrefragable arguments he offered in the Boston press against the sanctity of charter grants and in favor of free bridges and free enterprise can be found again in the learned opinion which Chief Justice Taney rendered in the Charles River Bridge case.

From among the foregoing Jacksonians, Major William B. Lewis is missing. He was one of Andrew Jackson's oldest and closest friends, a neighbor in

Tennessee, Second Auditor of the Treasury, and a resident with the General at the White House. He was an expert politician, adept in the manipulation and creation of "public opinion," but seems to have had no economic interest other than that of southern planter. He was the only cultivator of the soil, the only real agrarian, the President kept close to him in Washington, and he was of the well-to-do sort, not the horny-handed. He was also the only one of the President's closest associates to befriend the Bank of the United States. He seems to have thought it more sensible to make the Bank Jacksonian than to destroy it. His was the sole agrarian element in the administration's relations with the Bank, and it was not hostile. . . .

VI

Despite the fact of a strong and determined rebellion within the business world against the Bank of the United States, the fiction that the attack on the Bank was on behalf of agrarians against capitalists, of humanity against property, of the poor against the rich, and of "the people" against "the money power," has persisted. There was, to be sure, an extremely respectable minority comprising the more conservative and thoughtful men of business, Mr. Gallatin, for example, and Nathan Appleton, who defended the Bank till near the end, but it will scarcely do to say that they represented the business world while C. C. Cambreleng, David Henshaw, and Reuben Whitney did not.

It is obvious that New York, besides gaining most from a successful attack on the Bank, risked the least; for it did not need, as the South and West did, the capital brought in by the Bank's branches. The West's aversion for the federal Bank was like the nationalistic resentment in a 20th century under-developed economy which wants and needs imported capital but growls at the "imperialism" of the country that is expected to provide it. The western enemies of the Bank were moved by complex psychological and political considerations—including past distress and present dependence—while its New York enemies were moved, much more simply, by covetousness and rivalry. This was the decisive new ingredient provided in the Jacksonian attack. The agrarian prejudice had been alive since 1791 and most dangerous to the Bank a few years past during its critical days and the distress in the Ohio valley. The state bank opposition was almost as old as the agrarian. And the relative importance of the two varied with the decline of agrarianism and the growth of enterprise. New York, now the center of enterprise, added to the long-lived antagonism a hearty and acute self-interest. That Andrew Jackson proved to be the instrument of her interest was the happy result of Mr. Van Buren's skill and devotion.

It goes without saying that Andrew Jackson himself did not understand what was happening. He had started with a vague, agrarian prejudice against banking which on occasion cropped up throughout his life but never led him to deny himself the service of banks or the friendship and support of bankers. It was no great task for his advisers to arouse this dormant distrust, nourished on what he had read about the South Sea Bubble, and focus it upon the Bank in Philadelphia, a city whence he had suffered years before, at the hands of a bankrupt merchant and speculator, a harsh financial misfortune. Nor was an elaborate plot required to be agreed upon among conspirators. The first harassment of the Bank from the administration group was evidently spontaneous and simply aimed at making the Bank Jacksonian. Some time elapsed before it got under directed control. Even then there is no reason to suppose that the program was not mainly opportunistic. In the early stages the object need have been only to make sure that the charter be not renewed. To this end the General's mind must be fixed against the Bank, and the proper improvement of opportunities could be left to the discretion of those in whose path the opportunities appeared. The adviser who influenced the General most directly or who perhaps left the best record of what he did was Roger B. Taney, though he joined the Jacksonian circle late. He succeeded in filling the General's mind with a vindictiveness that Martin Van Buren or Amos Kendall would probably not have produced. They too would have killed the Bank but with less emotion and less cant. "When a great monied institution," Mr. Taney told the General, "attempts to overawe the President in the discharge of his high constitutional duties, it is conclusive evidence that it is conscious of possessing vast political power which it supposes the President can be made to feel." The Taney reasoning is sound, but the premises are misrepresented, and the effect was to fill the President with bitter suspicion of the Bank; though the alleged "attempts to overawe the President"—this was written in June 1832—were the reasonable attempts of Mr. Biddle to gain support for the Bank, find out what the scowls and rumblings from Washington signified, and remove the doubts that he thought were troubling the President.

But thanks to the sort of thing Mr. Taney kept telling him, the President by now had few doubts such as Mr. Biddle imagined. He was merely considering how best to proceed against the Bank. Replacement, he realized, was necessary, and for a long time he was fumbling over unintelligible projects to that end. One of these projects, which may be intelligible to those whose understanding has not been corrupted by some knowledge and experience of the subject, was described to James A. Hamilton, 3 June 1830. The President had in mind "a national bank chartered upon the principles of the checks and balances of our federal government, with a branch in each state, the capital apportioned agreeably to representation and to be attached to and be made subject to supervision of the Secretary of the Treasury." He recalls having shown Mr. Hamilton "my ideas on a bank project, both of deposit (which I think the only national bank that the government ought to be connected with) and one of discount and deposit, which from the success of the State Bank of South Carolina I have no doubt could be wielded profitably to our government with less demoralizing effects upon our citizens than the Bank that now exists. But a *national* Bank, entirely *national* Bank of deposit is all we ought to have: but I repeat a national Bank of discount and deposit may be established upon our revenue and national faith pledged and carried on by salaried officers, as our revenue is now collected, with less injury to the morals of our citizens and to the destruction of our liberty than the present hydra of corruption and all the emoluments accrue to the nation as part of the revenue." But these ruminations belonged merely to a period of waiting. As soon as a promising arrangement offered, the President acted. He ordered the federal funds removed from the Bank and put in the banks of his friends.

Besides contributing mainly, by this course, to a shift of the money market from Chestnut Street to Wall Street, the General contributed to the inflation, the speculation, and the various monetary evils which, with a persistent agrarian bias, he blamed on banks and paper money. There were plenty of men in his own party, among them better agrarians than himself, who would have cleared his vision and tried to, but the old gentleman preferred the sycophantic advisers who stimulated his suspicions and prejudices, blinded him to facts, confused him about the nature of the federal Bank's usefulness, diverted his attention from the possibility that it be amended and corrected instead of being destroyed, and allowed him to declaim the most ignorant but popular clap-trap.

Louis Hartz: THE AMERICAN DEMOCRAT: HERCULES AND HAMLET

Louis Hartz brings a refreshingly new perspective to the history of American political thought by means of a comparative analysis of European and American liberalism. He argues that the absence of feudal institutions led to the overpowering triumph of a liberal society in America. And it was a liberalism that was unique because America was reproducing the liberal ideas of Europe in a society which functioned without the social antagonisms of Europe. Hence, the American liberal has often been led into a career of philosophic confusion because he uses a European political vocabulary in an environment that does not have the social mechanisms of Europe. This confusion is particularly apparent in the Jacksonian period as the following selection indicates. Yet, somehow, in the midst of this confusion, American politics follows a course which is shaped by a liberal consensus that is grounded in the social fact that the American democrat is a liberal of the small-propertied type.

2. "ARISTOCRAT," FARMER, "LABORER"

AS the American democrat struggled to reconcile the conglomerate elements of Western society out of which he was built, he produced a scheme of social thought that reminds one of a house of mirrors: the more rooms you enter the more bewildered you get. Consider, first of all, the way in which he absorbed the land and the factory into the ethos of democratic liberalism. Americans take this so completely for granted, especially the liberal agrarianism of Jefferson, that it rarely occurs to them how remarkable it actually is. The role of the land in the politics of modern Europe

From *The Liberal Tradition in America* © 1955 by Louis Hartz. Reprinted by permission of Harcourt, Brace & World, Inc., pp. 119–142.

still needs much historical study, but one thing would seem to be fairly clear. When it was not without a philosophy, as was true in the case of the peasantry and the tenantry, save for sporadic anarchist dreams like those of Proudhon or frustrated yeomen dreams like those of Cobbett, its spokesmen were usually conservative thinkers: men like Disraeli and Bonald. Liberalism was associated with the towns. The Jeffersonian theory, making land the indispensable base of liberal democracy, is quite an American matter, which shows us, as Whitney Griswold has pointed out, how plastic the agrarian virtues of Aristotle are. Jefferson and Disraeli are agreed on many points. They agree that there is a peculiar goodness in the cultivation of the land, that industrial cities are dangerous things. But observe the way they differ: Disraeli sees the land as fostering an ancient feudal order and the towns as fostering democracy, while Jefferson sees the land as fostering democracy and the towns a quasi-feudal kind of social dependence. The only irony that is needed to round this situation out is that capitalist Whiggery is blasted either way: Bright is assailed from the right, Daniel Webster from the left.

But this is not the main point. The main point is that the democratic-liberal transformation of the land in America was not quite complete, for the great early Southern agrarians were large plantation magnates who cherished, as much as America permitted it, the aristocratic ethos. This is not true in the case of Jefferson, whose faith in "small landholders" as the "most precious part of the state" cannot be seriously questioned. John Taylor, however, is a case of another kind. It is not hard to see that he is a radical democrat only because he cannot be an authentic aristocrat: because the land in America is predominantly in the hands of small entrepreneurs and if he wishes to defeat the Hamiltonian program he must join with a democracy that shares his debtor complex. He himself admitted as much as this when he said that a "multitude of proprietors" had made the American land "irretrievably republican," so that an "aristocracy cannot exist," which meant that a gentleman had "no alternative" but to move to the political left. Here was a strange frustration: living on the radical edge of the Enlightenment only because you could not live on the conservative edge of the Reaction, supporting the independent farmer only because the "good discipline" of the English estate was impossible in a liberal world. What it meant, of course, was that the Mr. Hyde of an Edmund Burke was always struggling to explode beneath the Dr. Jekyll of a Thomas Paine. And eventually the explosion did in fact occur. When the tenants began to revolt in the Hudson Valley, James Fenimore Cooper, an "aristocrat," moved from blasting Whiggery's stake-in-society argument to supporting the good Burkian notion that the "column of society must have its capital as well as its base." In the South, where slavery made the liberalism of the "aristocrats" doubly dubious, the explosion was tremendous. When abolitionism got under way, John Taylor, transforming himself into George Fitzhugh, did his best to dream the dream of Scott and the European reaction.

Even if these strange tensions within the agrarian part of his personality had never been resolved, however, the American democrat would have had to face the problem of uniting to it the urban part of his personality. This was no minor task in the realm of psychic integration. Had it been concerned alone with absorbing petty urban traders, the classic Western base of his political personality, the task might not have been so hard. But important as these became in the Jacksonian era when American business grew increasingly democratic, they were by no means of crucial importance. The crucial group that had to be dealt with was the growing group of urban laborers: the very "mobs of great cities," in other words, that Jefferson no less than Disraeli feared with an ardent fear. If half of the American democrat believed that the "workshops" of Europe ought to "remain in Europe," how was the other half, grounded in those workshops, ever to get along with it?

This is a well-known problem. We know that Jefferson was ultimately forced to change his mind about the urban worker. We know that in the Jacksonian era men like Ellery Sedgwick tried hard to dispel the old Jeffersonian bias, emphasizing the new opportunities that towns opened, their social contribution. But what seems to me the important thing is something else: the nature of the error Jefferson made. For what Jefferson was doing when he assailed the industrial worker was overlooking the magical alchemy of American life which was responsible for the very small liberal farmers that he loved. That alchemy, in addition to transforming passive peasants into dynamic liberal farmers, was going to transform bitter proletarians into incipient entrepreneurs. Jefferson emphasized the concrete fact of the ownership of property, which to be sure was not a characteristic of the industrial worker. But this was a kind of Marxian mistake, emphasizing economics at the price of thought, for the French peasant also owned property and he was

far from being the enlightened liberal yeoman that Jefferson relied so heavily upon. The fact is, the liberalism of the American farmer was largely a psychological matter, a product of the spirit of Locke implanted in a new and nonfeudal world; and this spirit, freed as it was of the concept of class and the tyranny of ancient tradition, could infect the factory as well as it infected the land. There is no need in either case to underrate the importance of America's vast resources which produced, as Selig Perlman has put it, a "premise of abundance" hostile to the concept of class. But the ideological factor, the factor that Turner missed, is a matter of profound importance, and when Jefferson failed to understand it in the case of the urban worker he showed as well that he did not understand it in the case of the country farmer.

Jefferson's fear, in other words, was actually less real than the frustration of John Taylor. The American liberal world had a certain amount of pain to inflict on an "aristocratic" agrarianism as it confronted "small proprietors" but it had no pain to inflict on a democratic-liberal agrarianism as it confronted an urban working class. We need not now go over the familiar story, the lament of every Marxist, of how the early American labor movement stuck to the concepts of property and individualism. Stephen Skidmore, thrown out of the New York workingmen's party because of his radical educational schemes, wanted to guarantee inalienable the right of acquiring wealth. Orestes Brownson, certainly not the most moderate labor philosopher, dreamed of each worker being "an independent labourer on his own capital—on his own farm or in his own shop." Indeed the irony of Jefferson's fear of an urban "mob" is that he himself became its philosophic idol when it began to develop, and not merely in a general egalitarian sense: in the sense also of his theory of agrarian independence. The labor literature would not give up the old idea of yeoman free-holding, and when as with Lucius Byllesby it was recognized to be impossible in the East, it was rediscovered with George Henry Evans in the new lands of the West. Jefferson had reason enough before he died to modify his fear of the American working class.

But even though he modified it he never really undid all of the damage it inflicted on the growing personality of the American democrat. During the Jacksonian era, while labor writers were clinging to Jefferson's small propertied individualism, Whigs were actually citing Jefferson in their campaign against working-class suffrage. In other words, if the "aristocrat" could flee from the democrat, the agrarian democrat could stick a dagger into the urban democrat, and the centrifugal forces in American democracy could move in several directions at once.

We have, however, to relate this complexity of soul to the symbolism produced by the battle against Whiggery. Under almost any circumstances, given a strategic situation in which power was stacked on the side of the American democrat so long as Whiggery maintained an elitist policy which isolated it from the American liberal world, the American democrat was bound to assist in that isolation. In other words, he was bound to dramatize the differences between Whiggery and himself as starkly and as vividly as possible and thus to obscure what he had in common with it: what any liberal of small property has in common with any liberal of large

property, what the European shopkeeper has in common with the European industrialist. But being, precisely because of this strategic situation, a huge and various giant, an agrarian and a worker as well as a shopkeeper, the opportunities for confusing the American alignment were radically enhanced. I do not mean by this merely the opportunity he had, since no titled aristocracy existed, of blasting the Whigs as "aristocrats," a familiar polemical technique of the age, which is more than a bit incongruous when his own early leadership itself consists of frustrated Southern "aristocrats." When Taylor calls Hamilton an "aristocrat," it takes a moment or two to figure out what is going on. What I centrally have in mind is the way the American democrat dramatized himself as against both the "aristocrat" and "capitalist" labels that he applied to American Whiggery.

In the first place, being an agrarian, he proceeded at once to describe the battle between himself and the Whigs as a battle between "agrarians" and "capitalists." This antithesis, which we find as polemic in the work of Jefferson and Taylor and as sober historical writing in the work of Beard and Parrington, was excellently designed to draw a red herring across the track of the American democrat's own liberal capitalist character. In a battle between "agrarians" and "capitalists," if a man is an "agrarian," how can he be a "capitalist?" Here is a devilish confusion indeed. It is true, of course, that capitalism as a system of economy and as a way of life produced an urban industrialism, but the notion that "agrarianism" is a reasonable antithesis to it cannot be defended. English capitalism first appeared on the land, and the originators of modern capitalist economics, the physiocrats, were middle class members of the French bureaucracy who invaded the feudal setup and tried to imitate the English. Taylor, up to a point, was one of their disciples. A feudal ethos and a feudal tradition did, indeed, persist on the English land, producing Disraeli's conservatism, but it is the ethos and the tradition, not the land, which was antithetical to capitalism. And these, as we have seen, were exactly the things that were missing in America. That was why a Disraeli was a world apart from a Jefferson: the one had the feudal spirit, the other had the spirit of the small liberal entrepreneur.

One of the great ironies of America's class struggle between the "agrarian" and the "capitalist" is that with John Taylor it achieved the dignity of a historical philosophy. Taylor's historical theory is a kind of Marxism ending in a smashing anticlimax. The Roman masses overthrow the ancient aristocracy, the capitalists overthrow the feudal aristocracy, and capitalists are overthrown not by a propertyless proletariat but by a set of capitalist farmers. Of course Taylor is careful not to rank the American farmers with the capitalist men of "commerce," for this would expose the fact that the battle between him and Hamilton could be subsumed under one side of the battle between Locke and Filmer that preceded it: it would expose a sudden unity at precisely the time of apocalyptic conflict. But is it not obvious on the face of it that Taylor shared the property-owning, entrepreneurial ethos of Locke just as much as Hamilton did? Why else did he, and above all Jefferson, cherish the farmer and fear the "mob"? It was because the "mob," not as Marx but as everyone saw, was the true potential enemy of the capitalist.

But the American democrat did not belabor Whiggery merely by calling himself an "agrarian." He also called himself a "laborer." One might suppose that this was the result of the working-class component of his hybrid character, and hence would come into conflict with the theory of struggle produced on the rural side. The class struggle between "agrarian" and "capitalist," given the Jeffersonian fear of towns, ought not to be a convenient bedfellow for the class struggle between "laborer" and "capitalist." Actually, however, it was at this point that some accommodation between the two sides of the American democratic personality was theoretically made. For Taylor, in addition to defining himself as "agrarian," defined himself as a "laborer" —"my fellow laborers," as he put it—and thus shifted attention to a general struggle between men who produced and the "capitalists" who exploited men who produced. During the Jacksonian era this became a rock of the urban labor literature. George Bancroft, after asserting that "farmers are the true material for a republic," lauded also the laboring "manufacturer." He contrasted them both with the "man who does but exchange."

But the point made before has to be made again: did not the American farmer "exchange," the farmer that impressed Tocqueville so keenly with his speculative and entrepreneurial ambitions? And did not the American worker dream of doing so? Surely the latter instance is one of the greatest instances of confusion. The Marxist who is disappointed because of the "petit-bourgeois" nature of the early American labor movement is often comforted because he finds in its literature astonishing "anticipations of Marx," phrases of flashing insight into the nature of class struggle. At the very moment that the American worker betrays in a hundred ways his solidarity with the

Whigs on the liberal individualist principle, and hence his solidarity with the Jeffersonian agrarians who feared him as much as the Whigs did, he speaks of class war. Seth Luther, a Boston labor leader influenced by his participation in Dorr's Rebellion, even went so far as to "anticipate" the concept that no class peacefully gives up power: "In all cases," he wrote, "the people have been compelled to take by force that which has been withheld from them by force."

What all of this adds up to is fairly clear. The American liberal world practically led the small propertied liberal of America to a career of philosophic confusion. By making him, first of all, a huge and hybrid figure, he was never quite sure whether he was an "aristocrat," a farmer, or an urban worker, or whether in any of these roles he liked himself in the others. Then, by putting him as a result of this process into a strategic situation where Whiggery was his only opponent and the way to defeat it was to isolate it from him, it urged him to forget the liberal capitalism he shared with it and to concentrate on the new-found agrarianism and proletarianism of his social personality. The categories of farmer versus capitalist (aristocrat) and laborer versus capitalist (aristocrat) thus automatically appeared. And, of course, since the Whigs themselves, until around 1840, deliberately isolated themselves from the American democrat, fearing him, denouncing him, even persisting in the dream of an aristocratic alliance against him, the symbolism that he advanced served as a natural counterpart to the one that they advanced. William Leggett's attack upon the "capitalist" beautifully balanced Fisher Ames's attack upon the "mob." The liberalism of American life, by erecting a set of hidden traps and false façades, confounded not one group but all groups who lived within it. But insofar as the American democrat is concerned, this process reached its climax when, grappling with the issues raised by his own individualist fear and capitalist lust, he fell abjectly, confusedly, into the hands of the Whigs.

3. INDIVIDUALIST FEAR: THE PROBLEM OF THE MAJORITY

Being a liberal community, America, not unnaturally, has had as its central problem in political thought the classic liberal problem of majority rule and minority rights. What the issue of Enlightenment rationalism and feudal traditionalism has been for Europe the issue of majority rule has been for America, which shows us in a sense the relationship of American to European thought, for the reconciliation of majority rule and minority rights is an inner phase of the Enlightenment scheme. It is a problem which appears within the philosophy of Locke once his major premises have been granted. But though this has been the classic problem of American thought, it has rarely occurred to American thinkers that precisely for that reason there has been a classic solution to it: namely that when a nation is united on the liberal way of life the majority will have no interest in destroying it for the minority. Santayana, exploring America's "unison," caught at once the crucial fact that minorities on any issues could easily tolerate the outcome "either way." But the American perspective has not been Santayana's, and so the very liberalism that restrains the majority has given rise to a vast neurotic fear of what the majority might do. What must be accounted one of the tamest, mildest, and most unimaginative majorities in modern political history has been bound down by a set of restrictions that betray fanatical terror. The

American majority has been an amiable shepherd dog kept forever on a lion's leash.

But this has been a voluntary servitude and we must not assume, as our Progressive historians often imply, that it has been forced upon the American democrat by the subtle machinations of American Whiggery. Those machinations have taken place, but save for the cooperation of the American democrat himself, there is no reason why they should have been any more successful than the effort to limit suffrage through property qualifications. We are often told a story of the conquest of the American democrat by dark "capitalist" forces, which omits to explain how a man as powerful as he could be conquered against his will. In the last analysis it is Jefferson, not Hamilton, who is responsible for the harness in which Jefferson has been placed, and this is due to the fact that, missing the nature of American liberalism, he has shared to the full America's neurotic terror of the majority. In the case of Jefferson specifically, it is true, one has to qualify this remark. Amid his battle against "capitalists," "aristocrats," and the urban proletariat, he often had remarkable flashes of insight into the nature of the American community. When in his First Inaugural he said, "We are all Democrats, we are all Republicans," he got hold of something that was usually vouchsafed to him only in his days of foreign travel, and when in his correspondence with John Adams toward the end of his life he tried to explain to the latter that "here everyone owns property" or has a "sufficient interest in it" to guarantee its protection, he made explicit the nature of the mildness of the American liberal majority. But on the whole this is not the theme of Jefferson. His theme is one of conflict. And so, when he insists

that the "rights of the minority" are sacred, he leaves up in the air the problem of how the majority will be kept from constantly destroying them. This is the prelude to only one thing: binding the majority down by institutional restraints.

The American democrat, in other words, caught up in reverse in the class war subjectivism of Whiggery, has no way of finally answering the argument of Chancellor Kent. To be sure, he can give every answer but the final answer. He can hammer away at the inconsistency of accepting the liberal notion of equality and then excluding the masses from political power, the moral contradiction that everywhere in the West indicted the integrity of the Whigs. But once he has emancipated the majority morally, the empirical terror of Chancellor Kent, like a demon of the mind that will not die, confounds him at every turn. What if the majority does behave like a "mob"? In the midst of a war between "agrarians" and "capitalists" and "aristocrats," can the individual ever be really safe? The answer of course is that no such war is going on, that the Americans, as General Root said in New York, were "all of the same estate." But the remark of Root, like the reply of Jefferson to Adams, was something stung out of the American democrat in an off-guard moment of objectivity, and it contradicted the very polemical process by which he isolated the Whigs and destroyed them. Could William Leggett, who defended the majority against the oppression of "lordlings," seriously defend it also because it had comparatively little against its oppressors? Here was an ironic trap from which there was no escape: the successful political heroics of the American democrat moved in one direction, the solution of the majority problem moved in the other.

It is illuminating, and pathetic as well, to observe in several specific cases the agony with which the American democrat struggled with an issue that the blinders on his eyes prevented him from understanding. John Taylor tried to reason his fears away by saying that "a minority may live upon the labours of a majority" but that "a majority cannot subsist upon those of a minority." This argument, which drew no distinction between the French majority of 1789 and the American majority of 1800, was hardly satisfactory. A majority may not be able to live off the labors of a minority, but it can surely profit from them. The fear of Hamilton was not to be exorcised by pointing out that some work would have to be done by the mob in any case. Taylor was on far solider ground when he simply dismissed with contempt those who "suffer imagination to conjure up a tumultuous populace, discharging its fury upon life, liberty, and property." But this, alas, was the beginning of an analysis that someone else would have to end. Why would the American populace fail to be "tumultuous"? Clearly, because it had much in common with the man its opponents claimed it would destroy. Taylor was the last person who could possibly emphasize a point like this. In his theory the "aristocracy of the third age" was purely parasitic, and nothing less than its total annihilation was called for.

George Camp and Richard Hildreth skirted even closer to the real issue without touching it. Camp said that the majority was "an extremely fluctuating body," controlled in one moment by the threat of a new majority in another, and Hildreth said that it was limited by the realization that an oppressive act, operating "on the sympathies of the community," would deprive it of its power. These were partial insights. Fluctuating majorities are indeed a protection for the minority, but what makes them fluctuate? It is a community where deep social conflicts do not freeze them into a permanent position. Kent's mythical mob was just such a frozen majority, and in the South the fear of Calhoun was that the North was becoming one too. The Civil War, the only instance in American history when Camp's analysis broke down, showed in part that Calhoun was right. Hildreth's point about "sympathy," was of much the same type. Sympathy does not operate in all cases; it operates, as Hildreth's own Benthamite analysis should have shown him, only when groups have enough in common to identify with each other. Both Camp and Hildreth, to develop their arguments to their logical conclusion, would have had to challenge fundamentally the whole social war trend of American thought.

And so it happened that the American democrat was barred by his own philosophy from discovering America's peculiar solution to the problem of majority rule. In 1837, at the flood tide of Jacksonian democracy, the *Democratic Review* painfully confessed that the majority concept "has ever been the point of the democratic cause most open to assault, and most difficult to defend." The characteristic anguish, evasions, bold fronts, and sudden collapses that we find in American democratic thought on this issue are nowhere better illustrated than in the editorial which contained this lament. Heroically announcing, "We are opposed to all restraints on the free exertion of the popular will," it then proceeded to say "except those which have for their sole object the prevention of precipitate legislation." And then, when elucidating these, it confessed that the "division of power" had to be ranked among them. The institution of judicial

review, Hamilton's American "aristocracy," it conveniently left unmentioned.
We do not have to go very far to discover the psychic turmoil that lay behind this omission. On this issue the
American democrat was always taking
one step forward and two steps backward. Jefferson blasted judicial review as
"the despotism of an oligarchy." Taylor's
attack was even more vehement, and so
was Van Buren's, but in the end the work
of Marshall flourished, and the symbolism of Court and Constitution became a
national fetish.

There was one compensating factor,
however, inherent in this situation. If
the American democrat threw himself,
out of excessive terror, into the harness
of Whiggery, the fact that the terror was
excessive meant that the harness would
not be unbearable. If he did not need
the restraints that Hamilton devised for
a "mob," the fact that he was not a "mob"
meant that he could endure those restraints far more easily than any "mob"
could. If Taney's Supreme Court had
been able to settle the Civil War in the
Dred Scott case, one might justify the
restraints on the American majority in
terms of the frightful premise which produced them. But it could not. The nor-
mal American majority has been able to
endure these restraints precisely because
its social ambitions have been mild. A
false American fear, in other words, has
produced a fantastic American system of
checks, and the falsity of the fear, the
liberal unity of the nation, has permitted
those checks to survive. The European
wonders at two things in America: our
elaborate majoritarian controls, and our
marvelous moral agreement. Who can
ponder these two things for a moment
without detecting the neurotic obsession
and the objective reality which binds
them both together?

4. CAPITALIST LUST: CONSCIENCE AND APPETITE

In the last analysis there was probably
nothing which could have prevented the
American democrat from delivering himself up to Whiggery on the count of capitalist ambition. But it is still a fact that
the philosophy of social war that he
worked out in demolishing Fisher Ames
confounded again and again the process
by which he did so. Hidden hunger led
to betrayals that were even more inglori-
ous than those induced by hidden fear.
There was, of course, the deepest connection between these two passions: the
dream of new and greater wealth dou-
bled the desire to protect wealth in general, so that the acceptance of the Hamiltonian restraints was based, half-con-
sciously, on a judgment of the future,
Fear was a part of lust, and lust a part
of fear: the passion of the American
democrat was an integrated force. Where
trouble appeared was when it came into
conflict with his polemical super-ego of
"capitalists" and "aristocrats."

In the realm of economic policy, as if
social thought were not already confused
enough, another factor entered to con-
fuse further. This was the program of
state promotionalism that Whiggery in
America was forced to advance. Now this
program, as I have already said, was
largely traceable to the underdeveloped
nature of the American economy, and
had the American Whigs been in England they not only would not have had
to advance large parts of it, but fighting
the vestiges of a corporate society, they
would have become champions of laissez
faire. The corporate charter with limited liability, one of the greatest bones
of contention in America, was in England
actually the objective of the "smaller capitalists" whom John Stuart Mill defended,
men who wanted to compete with larger

entrepreneurs—the English counterparts of the American democrat if England can be said to have any. But despite this, the American democrat seized upon the promotional principle as the historic clue to the rise of the "capitalist." The result was that a theory of class war which in the first instance was overdrawn became further confounded by a theory of class causality which cannot be defended. To John Taylor's philosophy of capitalist farmers overthrowing "capitalists" must be added the additional ideal that the "capitalists" arise out of the political action of legislatures.

This notion, which Jefferson also had and which even Beard concedes "reverses the facts," easily arose in America for another reason as well. Starting with a comparatively free society, America had traditionally focused its fears upon the state, and so when the large capitalist began to emerge the instinctive American compulsion was to blame the state for him. The "reversal of the facts" that we find in American democratic thought was an extension of that preoccupation with the political conclusions of Locke which even in the eighteenth century the empirical nature of his social premises had made possible. Europe, on the other hand, starting with feudalism, could not miss the primacy of the social question. There the coercions of corporate society antedated the modern state, the state had been an instrument in their destruction, and the capitalist indeed had helped to destroy them. It is not accidental that the "capitalist" is for Taylor a pure villain while for Marx he is a hero and a villain at the same time. Nor is it accidental that the theorists in America who denounced most forcefully the Jeffersonian tendency to "reverse the facts" were the society-conscious followers of Fourier, men like Godwin and Brisbane, whose perspectives had been shaped in the atmosphere of Europe. The taken-for-granted social freedom of America had blinded it to the fact that society, just as much as politics, might be a source of evil.

Few things could be worse for the intellectual integrity of the American democrat than the identification of the "capitalist" and the "aristocrat" with the public action of legislatures. For when he himself began to adopt large parts of the Whig program, he was put in the position of grinding out the very demons who oppressed him. This is the awful irony that cuts through the career of the American democrat from the time of Jefferson onward—from the time Jefferson said that "what is practicable must often govern what is pure theory." It was worse than the silent acceptance of judicial review after denouncing it. There the American democrat merely submitted to an instrument of the "aristocrats," but here he actually created the "aristocrats" themselves. He could, to be sure, advance certain arguments in his behalf. He could say that his own charters and internal improvements served both the "high and the low," as Jackson once put it, and hence were an "unqualified blessing." He could fight for free incorporation, although this did not meet the argument Taylor advanced when, assailing the purchase of bank stock, he said that "every man may enlist in an army, yet an army may enslave a nation." But whatever his theoretical logic might be, the gap between theory and practice was striking. A Pennsylvania Whig sardonically asked of the Democrats in 1837: "Can it be possible that a party which believes banks to be monopolies can go on so rapidly creating them?" And a writer in the *Democratic Review*, in a moment of high humor, distinguished between "a Democrat by trade" and "a Democrat in principle." "Heaven forfend," he added, "that any son of mine should be a Democrat in principle—being a good Democrat by trade, he got a snug slice of the public deposites."

The clash between capitalist hunger and anticapitalist principle reached its climax, of course, on the banking question. Charles A. Dana, a disciple of the easy credit schemes of Proudhon, lamented that American democracy waged a "relentless war" on the banks of "discount and circulation" which the petit-bourgeois democracy of France realized to be in its own interest. But the war was more relentless in theory than in practice. Mr. Bray Hammond has told the story brilliantly. The hard-money dreams of Taylor and Jackson were shattered by rising entrepreneurs, Western farmers, and private bankers who favored the assault on Biddle not in order to limit credit but rather to expand it at the hands of local banks. This type of pressure had been exerted even against the First Bank of the United States under Jefferson. By the time of Jackson, America's "acquisitive democracy"—its "millions of go-getting Americans," as Hammond puts it—overwhelmed the concept of credit control. The speculative boom of the thirties is an excellent commentary on the get-rich-quick compulsion of the American democrat. A writer of the time, describing that boom, said: "A young man who went to any of our large cities penniless was considered a blockhead if he did not report himself worth one or two hundred thousand dollars in a few years." This is the sort of spirit that it is hard to reconcile with an attack on "capitalists."

Eighteen-forty, as well as the age of Whig supremacy after the Civil War which it foreshadowed, was in this sense not a break with the past but a continuation of it. The open enchantment of the American democrat with Whiggery when he followed Harrison was a logical extension of his secret enchantment with it when he demolished John Quincy Adams. And this is precisely what Orestes Brownson saw. As he watched the log-cabin enthusiasms of 1840, he was struck with a flash of historic insight. All along, it had been the people, the "proletary," who had been responsible for his miseries. It had been they who had created "the immense system of corporations," they who had sustained the "ruinous system of paper money," they who had contracted abroad some "two hundred millions of dollars" of public works and corporation debts. And indeed if one went back as far as Jefferson, "will anyone tell us" wherein his policy "differed essentially from that of Mr. Adams"? Brownson had discovered at last the nature of the American liberal world. But being a classic intellectual, he did not blame his theory: he blamed the world. And so we find him fleeing from the principle of democracy, embracing Catholicism and conservatism, insisting in 1853 that the "distinction of classes" was "permanent and indestructible" and that the slavery of the South was a positive good. One is reminded of the flight to conservatism on the part of intellectuals after the French Revolution in Europe. But there was this difference, inherent of course in the nature of things: in Europe the flight was due to an excess of radicalism; in liberal America Brownson's flight was due to the fact that there had not been enough. The disenchantment of the American intellectual has always been of an oddly inverted kind: ironically it has been hailed as proof that he is "European."

5. THE PROBLEM OF UNANIMITY

We come back to our central point: the weakness of the American democrat was a part of his strength, his defeat a part of his victory. America isolated Whiggery by making the entire nation as liberal as it was, and this was also the reason that the entire nation, in the end, fell for its liberal fears and its capitalist dreams. An instinct of friendship, as it were, was planted beneath the heroic surface of America's political conflict, so that the contenders in it, just as they were about to deliver their most smashing blows, fell into each other's arms. American politics was a romance in which the quarrel preceded the kiss.

The strange thing about this story, however, will always be the intricate mechanism of philosophic confusion by which it unfolded. Starting with the moment the Federalists are robbed of their liberal personality, deprived of the House of Lords they look for, and sent assailing a set of "levellers" that do not exist, and then moving through the time of the emergence of the American democrat, with his inner "aristocratic"-democratic, rural-urban tensions, and his philosophy of assailing "capitalists" and "aristocrats," and coming finally to the age of Whiggery's democratization and the collapse of the American democrat, the record of American political thought is a veritable jig-saw puzzle of theoretical confusion. But throughout it all the liberal temper of American theory is vividly apparent. Locke dominates American political thought, as no thinker anywhere dominates the political thought of a nation. He is a massive national cliché. And as always in American history, when the Americans glance for a moment abroad, and see lands where this is not so, they are seized by a new objectivity.

At the height of the Jacksonian "revolution," comparing America with Europe, James Fenimore Cooper said: "Every other enlightened nation of the earth is at this moment divided between great opposing principles; whereas here, if we except the trifling collisions of pecuniary interests, everybody is of the same mind except as to the ordinary immaterial question of a choice between men."

Here, I think, we find the clue to Croly's judgment on the political thought of the Middle Period: that it was sterile. Some of the very writers who produced it conceded as much. Brownson said that "no work on politics of the slightest scientific value" had yet been written by an American and that "all questions relating to the origin and ground of the State" were sneered at by men in politics. We cannot explain this fact, as George Camp tried to explain it at the time and as many have tried to explain it since, by saying that the Americans "had the forest to subdue, a new continent to occupy," and hence were too busy with material things to be political philosophers. The frontier, taken alone, no more explains the sterility of our political thought than it explains the speed of our democratic success. England during this same period unloosed immense material energies, pushing through an industrial revolution which reshaped the face of the nation, and yet largely because of that revolution it produced its Benthams, its Mills, and its Carlyles. When a nation has cause for political philosophy, nothing can stop it from producing it, and the clue to its absence in America lies in the absence of a cause. The absence of "opposing principles," the fact that beneath its political heroics the nation was of the "same mind" on the liberal formula, settled in advance the philosophic question.

But this in itself involves a problem: not the problem of the majority, which the Americans agonized themselves over so much, but the problem of virtual unanimity which, as Santayana saw, proved that their agony was excessive. It is interesting how this problem silently began to unfold beneath the heroic clashes of American Whiggery and American democracy. The collapse and transformation of the Whigs had this effect: it destroyed the only philosophy in America which, with the exception of the philosophy that the South produced in defense of slavery, enshrined the principle of diversity implicit in the principle of hier-

archy. If Burke was not to be found in America, Adams at least was. And if the latter cherished delusions on the right and delusions on the left, they contained at any rate some hint of a dream of social diversity. The log-cabin passions of Harrison made Whiggery more realistic, but they swept even this dream away, so that the common American ethic, the "opinion" that frightened Tocqueville, became the conscious symbol by which the nation lived. Once the Southern philosophic challenge was liquidated, the "Americanism" that lay behind the shadow world of the Middle Period would come into its own amid the applause alike of Carnegie and Brandeis.

Marvin Meyers: THE OLD REPUBLIC AND THE NEW

Marvin Meyers has added new dimensions to our understanding of the Jacksonian period. Using a method of close textual analysis of the literature in the Jacksonian dialogue, Meyers is able to probe more deeply into the hopes and fears, the passions and the beliefs which lay beneath the public language of politics. He finds the Jacksonians caught in an agonizing inner conflict as they tried to apply the moral rhetoric of the simpler social order of the Old Republic to a society drawn into a more rapid pace of economic development with all of its fascinating lures in new forms of acquisition, promotion, and speculation. The following selection is the introductory chapter in The Jacksonian Persuasion.

JAMES PARTON, that excellent popular biographer of his eminent countrymen, consulted a map in 1859 to discover which notables had given their names most frequently to American places. I doubt that one can find a better brief guide to relative popularity, and to

relative political significance for the people, than Parton's simple finding:

Washington ....198 times
Jackson 191
Franklin 136
Jefferson 110
Clay 42

Reprinted from *The Jacksonian Persuasion: Politics and Belief* by Marvin Meyers with the permission of the publishers, Stanford University Press. © Copyright 1957 by The Board of Trustees of The Leland Stanford Junior University, pp. 1–10.

Washington the founder; Jackson the defender; Franklin the practical preceptor; Jefferson the republican sage; and far below, Clay the adjuster and promoter.

To have routed British veterans at New Orleans and cleared a region for settlement in the Indian campaigns gave Andrew Jackson a strong initial claim to national attention; and the military style which made him Old Hickory, Old Hero, put the claim in its strongest terms. Yet there had to be more to account for the passionate involvement of men's loyalties with Jacksonian politics: there had been other generals, other battles, other colorful personalities. At first, the battlefield reputation was enough: the unfailingly acute Governor Ford of Illinois, an uneasy late Jacksonian, observed how eager politicians had flocked to the banner of "a popular and fortunate leader" in the early days. But Ford saw too, in the perspective of 1850, that Jackson had been the master figure of American political life during his two administrations and the eight years of his retirement, and that he "has since continued to govern, even after his death."

Jackson entered the presidency a national hero out of the West; he became the great partisan protagonist of his generation. No man of his time was at once so widely loved and so deeply hated. His blunt words and acts assumed the character of moral gestures which forced men to declare themselves, for or against. The movement we have come to call Jacksonian Democracy borrowed more than a powerful name; it projected into politics a fighting image of the man who would save the republic from its enemies. Exactly where and how Andrew Jackson and his party met is a question for biographers; but once joined, they excited and focused the concerns of a political generation. George Bancroft's memorial

panegyric, for all its Transcendental claptrap, comes to a truth about Jackson's political significance:

Before the nation, before the world, before coming ages, he stands forth the representative, for his generation, of the American mind. And the secret of his greatness is this: by intuitive conception, he shared and possessed all the creative ideas of his country and his time; he expressed them with dauntless intrepidity; he enforced them with an immovable will; he executed them with an electric power that attracted and swayed the American people.

From contemporary commentators to recent scholars there has been agreement upon initial facts: that politics substantially engaged the interest and feelings of American society; that Jacksonian Democracy was a large, divisive cause which shaped the themes of political controversy; that the second quarter of the nineteenth century is properly remembered as the age of Jackson. Here agreement ends. The limits of the subject are in dispute: Is Jacksonian Democracy to be considered primarily as an affair of party politics, or as a broad political, social, and intellectual movement? What message did Jacksonian Democracy carry to society, whom did it reach, what did it signify in the setting of the times? These are yet unsettled questions, for all the wealth of industry and talent spent upon them.

In one view of the subject, urban masses rise against a business aristocracy; in another, simple farming folk strike out at capitalist trickery; in still another, fresh forest democracy seeks liberation from an effete East. Some recent works discover at the heart of the movement hungry men on the make invading the positions of chartered monopoly. Some stress the strengthening of the presidency, or the heightening of nationalist sentiment. An older emphasis upon King Andrew, master damagogue, exploiting the gullibility of the masses for the sake of his own power, reappears in altered form—the shrewd politicos behind a popular hero learning to manage a new mass electorate by perfecting the organization and tactics of machine politics. Woven into many accounts are elements of the official Jacksonian version: the friends of limited and frugal government, equal rights and equal laws, strict construction and dispersed power, taking up from Jefferson the defense of the republic.

These are not all the theses; and each is, of course, far more formidable in its author's custody than I have made it out in quick review. My object is simply to suggest the variety of plausible interpretations, and to suggest further the gaps and conflicts that invite a new effort to order our knowledge of Jacksonian Democracy. Much remains to be learned from precise and limited studies of the movement and the period; but now, I think, the need is to keep the focus wide: to ask the small questions with constant reference to the large.

Accepting the conclusions of Jacksonian scholarship as so many diverse hints to be considered when occasion gives them relevance, I have undertaken a new reading of some familiar sources. Somehow Jacksonian Democracy communicated a message which touched off powerful political emotions. What was this message, and what conditions gave it force? The questions are not easily answered.

When the Jacksonian movement formed in the late 1820's America was far out upon a democratic course: political democracy was the medium more

than the achievement of the Jacksonian party. The Jacksonians proclaimed popular principles with but little more insistence than the Whig supporters of Harry of the West or Old Tip. For most of the country the Federalist conservatism of Hamilton or John Adams was stone dead: its ghost walked only in the speeches of Jacksonians trying to frighten honest citizens out of their opposition. Government by the people was largely a matter of consensus and of wont. Basic principles and institutions were firmly settled; only their legal elaboration—for example, in suffrage extension and the increase of elective offices—was recent and still in progress. There was some party conflict over details, none over the general democratic direction. The completion of a popular regime seemed to follow an unquestionable logic.

Indeed the most consequential political changes entered silently, without formal consideration or enactment: changes in the organization and conduct of parties. The winning of elections became to an unprecedented degree the business of professionals who managed powerful machines. On the surface such developments might suggest a bureaucratization of political life; in main effect, however, they brought a novel intimacy to the relation between the people and politics. The political machine reached into every neighborhood, inducted ordinary citizens of all sorts into active service. Parties tended to become lively two-way channels of influence. Public opinion was heard with a new sensitivity and addressed with anxious respect. The bureaucratic science of machine operation was effective only in association with the popular art of pleasing the many. As never before, the parties spoke directly, knowingly, to the interests and feelings of the public. The Jacksonians initiated much of the change in the instruments and methods of popular democracy; they adopted new party ways with a natural ease and competence which earned them some electoral advantage; the Whigs understandably resented their success, and quickly followed their example. Thus the new party democracy, like democracy in the abstract, was a common element of politics and raised no substantial public issues between Jacksonians and their rivals. At most, the less successful partisans carped at the more successful.

Under the new political conditions parties were alert to interests everywhere in society. One is tempted to think that Jacksonian Democracy found a major class constituency, identified its concrete needs, catered to them in its program, won the interested vote, and so became a great political force; and that the Whigs did much the same thing with opposite interests and policies. Unfortunately, the scheme breaks down at critical points. The chief Jacksonian policies— opposition to special corporate charters, hostility toward paper money, suspicion of public enterprise and public debt—do not patently contribute to the needs of a distinctive class following. The parties show some interesting marginal variations in their sources of support; none-theless—given the relatively loose class structure, the heavy concentration in the middle social ranks as then identified (farmers, mechanics, shopkeepers), the flexibility of careers and the mixture of interests—it seems clear that both parties must have reached broadly similar class constituencies to gain, as they did, only a little more or less than half the popular vote. In sum: social differences were subtly shaded and unstable; party poli-

cies were ambiguous in their probable effects upon group interests; and so no general and simple class difference appears in party preferences.

The flaws in this class-interest approach have provoked a reaction toward the view that the Jacksonian movement had no great insurgent mission. In this view, the parties were fraternal twins, devoted to the advancement of slightly varying business interests in a free economy, their essential similarity disguised by a series of practical quarrels which windy party leaders dressed up in a conventional grand rhetoric; the essential meaning of Jacksonian politics is found in the objective import of legal and institutional changes. But why did political language go so far beyond practical objects? Why did men respond out of all proportion to their manifest interests? How were they convinced that party differences were profound, persistent—mattered greatly? Why did some kinds of rhetoric touch the quick, others not? Here, as elsewhere, the revisionist temper seems too impatient with the impalpable motives, feelings, perceptions, which lie between external act and external consequences.

I have spoken of the sensitive relationship which developed between parties and people: not only interests but attitudes and feelings reached the receptive eye of politicians. And politics took on what might be called an expressive role, along with its traditional task of conducting the business of the state. Here one enters a region of elusive psychological fact buried in a fragmentary record of words and acts. But here I think the vital transaction between Jacksonians and their generation must be found.

The appeals of the Democracy were carried by ideas and rhetoric, by policies and public gestures. Taken singly, these elements point this way and that, and no one of them conveys a full notion of the party message that worked such large effects. Taken together, I think, they converge to form an urgent political message with a central theme. It will be my purpose to identify that theme and the nature of its appeal. "Ideology" is a conventional term for one aspect of my subject, "ethos" for another, but I have chosen the less formal "persuasion" to fit my emphasis upon a matched set of attitudes, beliefs, projected actions: a half-formulated moral perspective involving emotional commitment. The community shares many values; at a given social moment some of these acquire a compelling importance. The political expression given to such values forms a persuasion.

In Jacksonian political appeals I have found—as might be expected—distinct traces of every theme used by historians to explain the nature and import of Jacksonian Democracy. Jacksonian spokesmen drew upon an exhaustive repertory of the moral plots which might engage the political attention of nineteenth-century Americans: equality against privilege, liberty against domination; honest work against idle exploit; natural dignity against factitious superiority; patriotic conservatism against alien innovation; progress against dead precedent. A first ungraded inventory shows only a troubled mind groping for names to fit its discontent.

The great specific mission of Jacksonian Democracy was the war against the Monster Bank. Here the party formed, or found, its character. Here was the issue which stood for all issues. Broad popular fear and hatred of the Second Bank, evoked by Jacksonian appeals, cannot be understood simply as a matter-of-fact reaction to material injuries. The economic

operations of the institution conferred some manifest general benefits, directly crossed the interests of only a limited group: its hand was not found upon men's throats or in their pockets. The Bank was called a Monster by Jacksonians. A monster is an unnatural thing, its acts are out of reason, and its threat cannot be estimated in ordinary practical terms. The effort to destroy the Monster Bank and its vicious brood—privileged corporations, paper money—enlisted moral passions in a drama of social justice and self-justification.

Broadly speaking, the Jacksonians blamed the Bank for the transgressions committed by the people of their era against the political, social, and economic values of the Old Republic. The Bank carried the bad seed of Hamilton's first Monster, matured all the old evils, and created some new ones. To the Bank's influence Jacksonians traced constitutional impiety, consolidated national power, aristocratic privilege, and plutocratic corruption. Social inequality, impersonal and intangible business relations, economic instability, perpetual debt and taxes, all issued from the same source.

Jefferson had brought into temporary equilibrium the formal ideal of a dynamic liberal society and the concrete image of a stable, virtuous yeoman republic. "It is," he wrote, "the manners and spirit of a people which preserve a republic in vigor." And God had made the independent citizen farmer "His peculiar deposit for substantial and genuine virtue." Nothing is more revealing than Jefferson's later concession of the need for domestic manufacturing, under the pressures of war: "Our enemy has indeed the consolation of Satan on removing our first parents from Paradise: from a peaceful agricultural nation he makes us a military and manufacturing one." Now Jacksonian society was caught between the elements—the liberal principle and the yeoman image—and tried again to harmonize them. Americans were boldly liberal in economic affairs, out of conviction and appetite combined, and moved their world in the direction of modern capitalism. But they were not inwardly prepared for the grinding uncertainties, the shocking changes, the complexity and indirection of the new economic ways. Their image of the good life had not altered: somehow, as men and as a society, they hoped to have their brave adventures, their provocative rewards, their open-ended progress, and remain essentially the same. The practical outcomes of the free pursuit of economic interest had never been legitimated, or even fully associated with the abstract liberal principle. Yet the ideological and material attachment to the liberal code was too deep to be severed, even in considerable distress.

Thus many found in the anti-Bank crusade, and in the Jacksonian appeal generally, a way to damn the unfamiliar, threatening, sometimes punishing elements in the changing order by fixing guilt upon a single protean agent. A laissez-faire society with this source of corruptions cut out would re-establish continuity with that golden age in which liberty and progress were joined inseparably with simple yeoman virtues. Under the Jacksonian persuasion men could follow their desires, protest their injuries, affirm their innocence. In this direction one can begin to meet the Jacksonian paradox: the fact that the movement which helped to clear the path for laissez-faire capitalism and its culture in America, and the public which in its daily life eagerly entered on that path, held nevertheless in their political con-

science an ideal of a chaste republican order, resisting the seductions of risk and novelty, greed and extravagance, rapid motion and complex dealings.

The Jacksonian movement was forged in the Bank War. Its new machine carried its influence throughout American society; its Old Hero, at once the voice and the exemplar of Jacksonian values, linked the machine to the essential cause. However far Jacksonians went in adapting policies to the practical requirements of local conditions, special interests, and effective party operation, the movement continually returned to its core appeal: death to the Monster; life and health to the old republican virtues. However carefully the knowledgeable voter looked to his immediate interests—when they could be linked plausibly to party policies—he would always see the moral choice proposed by Jacksonian Democracy.

If the Jacksonian persuasion gained relevance and force from common social experience, common tradition, how then did the Whigs develop a distinct voice and a substantial following? Reducing a complex matter to the utmost simplicity: the Whig party spoke to the explicit hopes of Americans as Jacksonians addressed their diffuse fears and resentments. To say this is to reverse a common historical appraisal. The Federalists had been, at the end, a party of fear and resentment. There is some loose justice in deriving Whiggery from Federalism; but only if one recognizes that the language of mob terror and elite guidance had gone out of general use before Jacksonians and Whigs assumed political leadership. Some unregenerate Federalists who worried openly about the dangers of extreme democracy still survived; Whig party leaders tapped them for campaign funds and otherwise wished them out of sight.

What the Whigs deliberately maintained in the inheritance was the ambitious scheme for economic progress through banks, tariffs, and public promotion of internal improvements. Clay's American System, the nearest approach to a coherent Whig policy, was a popularization of Hamiltonian economic designs and John Marshall's flexible interpretation of national authority. Whigs, too, fully associated themselves with the Old Republican idyll—Webster wept in memory of his father's forest hut; zealous clerks helped to clutter city streets with Harrison log cabins—but they felt no serious tension between past and present. Their cabin was a nostalgic prop, a publicity gimmick without focused moral content. The fulfillment of liberal premises in capitalist progress was for them entirely natural and unproblematic.

The Whigs distinctively affirmed the material promise of American life as it was going; and they promised to make it go faster. They were inclined to see the corporation not as a nameless monster but as an engine of progress; public debt not as a curse on honest labor but as a sound gamble on a richer future. Ironically, depression gave them their greatest popular success; yet they did not take depression as an omen of profound social maladjustment. They could see only that an imperious demagogue with primitive economic notions had thrown society into crisis by his spiteful war against the Bank. Indeed the Whigs were so markedly an anti-Jackson coalition that often their positive message was obscured in mere personal invective. To some degree, perhaps, the Whigs did succeed in spreading the conviction that Jacksonian dictatorship menaced the integrity of the republic. Principally, however, the party appealed to interested hopes, offering concrete advantages to groups and sections, and a quickening of economic progress for society as a whole.

Suggestions for Additional Reading

There are many works written by the Jacksonian generation that deserve to be read if they are available. William M. Gouge, *A Short History of Paper Money and Banking in the United States* (New York, 1835) reveals more about Jacksonian ideas than the title suggests. A useful collection of the editorials of William Leggett, the Jacksonian editor, is available in Theodore Sedgewick, Jr., *A Collection of the Political Writings of William Leggett* (New York, 1840). James Fenimore Cooper's *The American Democrat* (Vintage ed., New York, 1956) contains the reflections of America's leading novelist, who was both attracted to and repelled by Jacksonian democracy. Ralph Waldo Emerson's essays on *Politics* and on *New England Reformers* are also important pieces of political criticism and may be found in any of the numerous editions of Emerson's prose works. Thomas Hart Benton's *Thirty Years' View*, 2 vols. (New York, 1854–56) is a vigorous history of the times by a stalwart Jacksonian leader. Also useful is Martin Van Buren, *Inquiry into the Origins and Course of Political Parties in the United States* (New York, 1867). Thurlow Weed, *Autobiography*, edited by Harriet H. Weed (Boston, 1883), gives us valuable insights into the new style of politics from a Whig point of view. A very useful collection of representative writings by Jacksonians can be found in Joseph L. Blau, *Social Theories of Jacksonian Democracy* (New York, 1954).

The commentaries on Jacksonian America by Tocqueville, Martineau, and Grund should be read in their entirety for a more complete understanding of European perspectives. An excellent new edition of Michael Chevalier, *Society, Manners and Politics in the United States: Letters on North America* (Anchor ed., New York, 1961), is available and should be consulted for descriptions of industrial and transportation developments in America.

The works by Turner, Schlesinger, Hammond, and Meyers already noted in this volume are indispensable for further inquiry into the nature of Jacksonian democracy. Lee Benson raises many searching questions about the meaning of Jacksonian democracy in *The Concept of Jacksonian Democracy, New York as a Test Case* (Princeton, 1961). For a comprehensive account of the politics of the Jacksonian period, see Glyndon G. Van Deusen, *The Jacksonian Era* (New York, 1959). John W. Ward has made a brilliant analysis of the symbolic role of Andrew Jackson in *Andrew Jackson, Symbol for an Age*. The best study of the Presidency in the Jacksonian generation is Leonard D. White's *The Jacksonians, A Study in Administrative History, 1829–1861* (New York, 1956). The early chapters in Mosei Ostrogorski, *Democracy and the Party System in the United States* (New York, 1926) contain a good analysis of the new techniques of politics.

No one can understand the Jacksonian generation without investigating the basic social changes that were taking place at the time. The best study of the changing economic order is George Rogers Taylor, *The Transportation Revolution* (New York, 1951). For the economic ideas of the period one should consult Joseph Dorfman, *The Economic*

Mind in American Civilization, Vol. II (New York, 1946). Alice Felt Tyler's *Freedom's Ferment, Phases of Social History to 1860* (Minneapolis, 1944), is a comprehensive account of the utopian and humanitarian reforms of the period. Carl Russell Fish, *The Rise of the Common Man, 1830–50* (New York, 1929), contains useful information on the changes in art, education, religion, and science which accompanied the changes in the economic and social order. Vernon L. Parrington's *The Romantic Revolution* (Vol. II of Main Currents in American Thought, New York, 1927) can still be read with pleasure and profit.

The biographies of leading men in the Jacksonian period are too numerous to list in any complete fashion. John Spencer Bassett's *The Life of Andrew Jackson,* 2 vols. (New York, 1911), has not been surpassed by later biographers in scholarship or balanced judgment. Clement Eaton has written a perceptive treatment of Clay's role in American Whiggery in the brief book *Henry Clay and the Art of American Politics* (Boston, 1957). Richard Current did the same for Daniel Webster in *Daniel Webster and the Rise of National Conservatism* (Boston, 1955). Charles M. Wiltse's *John C. Calhoun,* 3 vols. (Indianapolis, 1944–51) is well written and contains much information on the general political history of the period.

Many excellent articles on the Jacksonians are available in such scholarly journals as *The American Historical Review, The Mississippi Valley Historical Review, The Political Science Quarterly,* and *The American Quarterly.* Charles Grier Sellers has written an excellent article on Jacksonian historiography, "Andrew Jackson versus the Historians," *Mississippi Valley Historical Review* (March, 1958), XLIV, pp. 615–648. In this connection, one should also consult John A. Ward's essay on "The Age of the Common Man" in John Higham, *The Reconstruction of American History* (New York, 1962).